LETTING GO OF ANXIETY AND DEPRESSION

WINDY DRYDEN was born in London in 1950. He has worked in psychotherapy and counselling for over 25 years, and is the author or editor of over 140 books, including *How to Accept Yourself* (Sheldon Press, 1999) and *Overcoming Envy* (Sheldon Press, 2002). Dr Dryden is Professor of Psychotherapeutic Studies at Goldsmiths College, University of London.

Overcoming Common Problems Series

For a full list of titles please contact
Sheldon Press, Marylebone Road, London NW1 4DU

The Assertiveness Workbook
A plan for busy women
JOANNA GUTMANN

Birth Over Thirty Five
SHEILA KITZINGER

Body Language
How to read others' thoughts by their gestures
ALLAN PEASE

Body Language in Relationships
DAVID COHEN

Cancer – A Family Affair
NEVILLE SHONE

Coping Successfully with Hayfever
DR ROBERT YOUNGSON

Coping Successfully with Migraine
SUE DYSON

Coping Successfully with Pain
NEVILLE SHONE

Coping Successfully with Your Irritable Bowel
ROSEMARY NICOL

Coping with Anxiety and Depression
SHIRLEY TRICKETT

Coping with Breast Cancer
DR EADIE HEYDERMAN

Coping with Bronchitis and Emphysema
DR TOM SMITH

Coping with Chronic Fatigue
TRUDIE CHALDER

Coping with Depression and Elation
DR PATRICK McKEON

Curing Arthritis Diet Book
MARGARET HILLS

Curing Arthritis – The Drug-Free Way
MARGARET HILLS

Depression
DR PAUL HAUCK

Divorce and Separation
Every woman's guide to a new life
ANGELA WILLANS

Everything Parents Should Know About Drugs
SARAH LAWSON

Good Stress Guide, The
MARY HARTLEY

Heart Attacks – Prevent and Survive
DR TOM SMITH

Helping Children Cope with Grief
ROSEMARY WELLS

How to Improve Your Confidence
DR KENNETH HAMBLY

How to Interview and Be Interviewed
MICHELE BROWN AND GYLES BRANDRETH

How to Keep Your Cholesterol in Check
DR ROBERT POVEY

How to Pass Your Driving Test
DONALD RIDLAND

How to Start a Conversation and Make Friends
DON GABOR

How to Write a Successful CV
JOANNA GUTMANN

Hysterectomy
SUZIE HAYMAN

The Irritable Bowel Diet Book
ROSEMARY NICOL

Overcoming Guilt
DR WINDY DRYDEN

The Parkinson's Disease Handbook
DR RICHARD GODWIN-AUSTEN

Talking About Anorexia
How to cope with life without starving
MAROUSHKA MONRO

Think Your Way to Happiness
DR WINDY DRYDEN AND JACK GORDON

Overcoming Common Problems

Letting Go of Anxiety and Depression

Dr Windy Dryden

sheldon PRESS

First published in Great Britain in 2003 by
Sheldon Press
1 Marylebone Road
London NW1 4DU

British Library Cataloguing-in-Publication Data

A catalogue record for this book is available from the British Library

ISBN 0–85969–893–9

1 3 5 7 9 10 8 6 4 2

Typeset by Deltatype Limited, Birkenhead, Merseyside
Printed in Great Britain by Biddles Ltd
www.biddles.co.uk

Contents

Preface

If you ask any counsellor, psychotherapist or clinical psychologist what are the two main problems that people seek help for, they will reply without hesitation: anxiety and depression. Thus, it seemed to me to be sensible to take note of this clinical reality and devote a book to these twins of human suffering. My goal is ambitious: to present in a short volume a number of guidelines that you can use to help yourself let go of anxiety and depression. It may be that you only suffer from one of these common psychological problems. Fine; if this is the case, read the first chapter, which lays the foundations of Rational Emotive Behaviour Therapy (REBT), the therapeutic approach on which this book is based, and then follow the specific guidelines that are presented in the chapter that is relevant to you (Chapter 2 for anxiety; Chapter 3 for depression). Because I realize that you may have bought this book because you want specific help with one of these emotional problems, I have used a very similar chapter structure for both problems. If you suffer from both conditions then you will want to read the book in its entirety, and I hope you will find it comforting that I have employed a very similar chapter structure in Chapters 2 and 3.

A word about terminology. You will note that I use the phrase 'letting go' of anxiety and depression throughout this book. This is what I mean by it. First, it is not humanly possible for you to be free from experiencing anxiety or depression again even after you have read, digested and acted on the ideas presented in this book. This will be the case even if you are very diligent in your implementation of these ideas. If this is your goal, in all probability you will fail. Second, none of us are blank slates when we are born. We are, of course, influenced to a large degree by our early experiences in our formative years, but we also have a biological heritage. We are born with inherited tendencies, which means that we are more likely to experience certain emotions than others who do not have such tendencies or who have them to a much weaker degree. Thus, I am pretty sure that I have an inherited tendency to make myself angry at life's frustrations, particularly when I am under pressure. My father is like this; so is his brother as was their father, my paternal grandfather. On the other hand, I rarely depress myself. I once really tried to get myself into a depressed state. I focused on all of my failures, withdrew from enjoyable activities, didn't get dressed or washed and listened to the depressing dirges of Leonard Cohen. I failed unmiserably! All I felt was a bit tired. Why did I fail? I believe because my inherited tendency to depress myself is quite weak.

If I am right about the importance of nature as well as nurture in the development and maintenance of the emotional disorders, what does this mean about the extent to which you can let go of anxiety and/or depression if you have a strong inherited tendency for either emotion or for both? Well, in my view the stronger your inherited tendency towards anxiety and/or depression, the more persistent you need to be in using the methods to be described in this book. If you do this you will be able to let go of your anxiety and/or depression as much as you are able, given your inherited tendency. Many people resist the idea of having an inherited tendency because they think that it means there is nothing they can do to help themselves. I hope you can see that I am not, I repeat *not*, advocating such a pessimistic view. I am taking the realistic position that (1) you may have an inherited tendency towards anxiety or depression (or even both) and if this is the case (2) you can still do a great deal to help yourself by working hard to deal with your anxious and/or depressed feelings by using the methods in this book. It is very unlikely that you will reach a stage where you will never make yourself anxious and/or depressed again. What you will achieve is relative freedom from these debilitating emotions, or what I call 'letting go' of anxiety and depression.

Finally, if you read this book, are dedicated and persistent in implementing the methods of REBT and yet make minimal progress, contact your GP. It is quite possible that you need professional help and/or medication to help you use the methods more effectively. Ask your GP for an opinion about taking medication and ask for a possible NHS referral to see an REBT or CBT (cognitive-behaviour therapy) practitioner. For a list of REBT therapists working in the private sector send an SAE to:

Association for Rational Emotive Behaviour Therapy
PO Box 39207
London
SE3 7XH

As ever, I invite you to write to me c/o Sheldon Press to tell me of your experiences of using this book in helping you deal with your own anxiety and/or depression problems. Good luck!

Windy Dryden
London and Eastbourne

1
Laying the Foundations

In this chapter I will lay the foundations for the following two chapters in which I show you how you can let go of anxiety (Chapter 2) and depression (Chapter 3). As I discussed in the preface, I have used the phrase 'letting go' advisedly throughout this book since, for the reasons that I explained in the preface, it is not possible for us as humans to overcome our problems once and for all.

The primary purpose of this chapter is to introduce the main ideas that you need to grasp if you are to get the most out of this book. First, I will present and expand on this book's major idea. It is that we disturb ourselves about life's adversities – real and imagined – by the rigid and extreme beliefs that we hold about these adversities. It follows from this idea that these negative life events do not directly disturb us. They contribute to our disturbance, to be sure, but they do not directly cause it. Thus, if we wish to un-disturb ourselves, as it were, about these events, we can most effectively do so by taking the rigidity and extremity out of our beliefs. You will see from the way that I introduce this idea – which is the backbone of Rational Emotive Behaviour Therapy, an approach to counselling and psychotherapy that was originally pioneered by Dr Albert Ellis – that I see holding rigid and extreme beliefs, on the one hand, and flexible and non-extreme beliefs, on the other, as a choice. Once you have made this initial choice – say, to hold flexible and non-extreme beliefs instead of their rigid and extreme counterparts – a lot of work is needed before these new beliefs become an integral part of your belief system.

The second point that I will discuss in this chapter is that when we take the rigidity and extremity out of our beliefs and we are left with holding flexible and non-extreme beliefs about life's adversities – real and imagined – we will still experience negative emotions about the negative events in our lives. The difference is that these negative emotions will be healthy and help us to deal as effectively as we can with life's adversities. This is why I call these emotions 'healthy negative emotions'. As such, they compare favourably with the disturbed negative emotions that stem from the rigid and extreme beliefs we hold about life's adversities. These unhealthy negative emotions, as I call them, interfere with our ability to deal effectively with life's adversities and often create more problems for us. So, when I speak of helping you to let go of anxiety and depression, I do not also imply that I will help you to achieve relative freedom from their healthy counterparts. It is healthy to feel bad when bad events happen. On the other hand, it is not healthy to feel disturbed when bad events happen. So, strange as it may seem at first sight, my goal in this book is to help you to feel bad when bad things happen to you – bad, but not disturbed!

To disturb yourself or not to disturb yourself? That is the question

Imagine this scenario. You have been charged with the responsibility of teaching a group of older children a philosophy of good mental health, principles which, if adopted and lived by, would help them to deal effectively with the slings and arrows of outrageous fortune and to move along the road towards self-actualization. You have just one constraint. You can only teach these children four principles.

How do you approach your task? After some thought you decide to review the literature of the world's greatest psychotherapists to see what they have to say about the subject. However, you don't have the time to do this. You just have time to choose the writings of one such therapist and hope you can find what you are looking for there. But whom do you select? There are just so many leading therapists to choose from. So you decide to let chance decide. You put the names of the world's leading therapists into a hat and draw – Albert Ellis, the originator of Rational Emotive Behaviour Therapy (REBT), whose ideas form the basis of this book.

Now what does Albert Ellis say about helping people to develop good mental health? Let me address this by giving you a series of choices.

Choice 1 Full preferences vs demands

REBT theory distinguishes between a full preference and a demand. Let me outline and illustrate each one before you choose which you would teach to your group of children.

A full preference is a belief where, when you hold it, you assert what you truly want but you do not demand that you have to have it. Thus, a full preference is flexible, whereas when you hold a demand you believe that you have to have what you want. This makes a demand rigid. Let me start by outlining how you might teach children about full preferences.

Children, as you live your life you will have many desires. You will want certain things to happen and you will want other things not to happen. Don't be ashamed of what you want or wish for. Being aware of your desires is a very important part of being human. However, as important is learning the following lesson:

Just because you want something to happen doesn't mean that it has to happen. And just because you want something not to happen doesn't mean that it mustn't happen.

Sometimes you get your desires met and sometimes you don't. And because you don't always get what you want and sometimes get what you don't want, it is important that you develop an attitude that reflects this fact of life. The best way of doing this is for you to keep in mind two important points that you need to combine into one belief: acknowledge that you want something, but also accept that there is no law that dictates that you have to get what you want.

Let me show you how to do this with respect to one of your desires for something to happen. Let's suppose that you want to go to university when you grow up. There is, of course, nothing wrong with this desire, assuming it is something that you truly want for yourself and not something that you don't want, but are doing for other people. This desire will motivate you to work hard for something that is important to you. However, just because you want to go to university, it doesn't follow that it is essential for you to get this desire met. You don't have to go to university even though it is important for you to do so. While at first glance it might seem that this component will stop you from trying to get into university, this isn't the case. It will, in all probability, stop you from being anxious and won't interfere with your striving to get what you want. Thus, your desire will motivate you, and your realization that it isn't essential to get what you want will help prevent you from being anxious as you work to achieve your goal.

So, children, to sum up: acknowledge what you want, strive for it if it is in your best interests to do so and accept that just because you want something, it doesn't mean that it is essential for you to get it.

Now, let me outline how you might teach children about demands.

> Children, as you live your life you will have many desires. You will want certain things to happen and you will want other things not to happen. When your desires are strong, you will be tempted to believe that it is absolutely necessary to have these desires met. Give in to this temptation. Convert your desires into absolute necessities. Tell yourself that because you want something to happen, it has to happen. And tell yourself that because you want something not to happen, it must not happen.
>
> Let me show you how to do this with respect to one of your desires for something to happen. Let's suppose that you want to go to university when you grow up. If this is important to you, tell yourself not only that you want to go to university, but that you have to go to university, it is absolutely essential for you to do so. Now there is a downside to converting your desires into absolute necessities and you should be aware of this downside before deciding whether or not to convert your desires into demands. Your desire to go to university will motivate you to work hard for something that is important to you. If you convert this desire into a demand and believe that you must go to university no matter what, you may work even harder and do so to the exclusion of everything else. You may even get obsessed about going to university. On the other hand, when you convert your desire into a demand, you may get anxious and this may stop you from working productively on your studies. This is the price that you pay for converting your desires into demands.
>
> So, children, to sum up: acknowledge what you want and convert your strong desires into demands. You run the risk of becoming emotionally disturbed if you do so, but this can't be helped.

You now know the difference between a full preference and a demand. Which of these two principles would you choose to teach to your group of children?

In your reading of Albert Ellis's work you quickly see that he holds that full preferences are at the core of psychological health and that the three other healthy beliefs that I am going to present to you – non-awfulizing beliefs, high frustration tolerance beliefs and acceptance beliefs – frequently stem from these full preferences. Similarly, you quickly learn that Ellis holds that demands are at the core of psychological disturbance and that the three other unhealthy beliefs that I am going to discuss – awfulizing beliefs, low frustration tolerance beliefs and depreciation beliefs – frequently stem from these demands. While you understand that other REBT therapists have different views on this subject, you decide to go along with the Ellis position in order to present the children that you have been charged to teach with a consistent viewpoint.

Choice 2 Non-awfulizing beliefs vs awfulizing beliefs

Ellis distinguishes between a non-awfulizing belief and an awfulizing belief. Let me outline and illustrate each one before you again choose which you would teach to your group of children. As I do so, remember that a non-awfulizing belief derives from a full preference and an awfulizing belief derives from a demand.

When you hold a full preference and desire, but do not demand, something then you are likely to hold a non-awfulizing belief when your desire is not met. A non-awfulizing belief asserts that it is bad when your desire is not met, but that it is not the end of the world, terrible or awful. A non-awfulizing belief is therefore non-extreme in nature, whereas when you hold a demand and your demand is not met, you are likely to hold an awfulizing belief where you assert that it is the end of the world, terrible or awful when your demand is not met. An awfulizing belief is therefore extreme in nature. Let me start by outlining how you might teach children about non-awfulizing beliefs.

> Children, as I have told you, in life you will have many desires. I have explained to you that it is important that you do not transform these desires into necessities and that you do not demand that you must get what you want. This will help you to respond constructively when you don't get what you want. When this happens, it is important that you learn this second lesson:
>
> *When you don't get what you want and you don't demand that you have to get it, consider this situation to be bad, unfortunate, but not the end of the world, terrible or awful.*
>
> When you hold a non-awfulizing belief you acknowledge that something can always be worse and that good can come from not getting what you want. Thus, when you want to go to university, but do not demand that you must do so, you acknowledge that it would be bad if you did not get into university, but you recognize that far worse could happen to you, and you also realize that if you failed to get into university, it would be possible for you to turn this to your advantage.

> So, children, to sum up: when you want something, but do not demand that you have to get it, remind yourself that it is bad when you don't get what you want. However, keep in mind that it isn't awful not to get what you want and that worse could happen to you. Also, remember that good can come from not getting what you want.

Now, let me outline how you might teach children about awfulizing beliefs.

> Children, I have already said that when your desires are strong, you will be tempted to believe that it is absolutely necessary to have these desires met. I urged you to give in to this temptation and convert your desires into absolute necessities. When you do so and you don't get what you believe you must get, tell yourself that it is the end of the world, terrible or awful.
>
> When you hold an awfulizing belief you acknowledge that nothing can be worse and that no good can possibly come from this situation. Thus, when you believe that you must get into university, you will tend to think that it would be awful if you didn't, and that you could not possibly turn this to your advantage since nothing good could possibly come from this state of affairs.
>
> So, children, to sum up: when you demand that you have to get what you want, remind yourself that it is the end of the world when your demand is not met, that nothing could be worse and no good could possibly come from your unmet demand.

You now know the difference between a non-awfulizing belief and an awfulizing belief. Again, which of these two principles would you choose to teach to your group of children?

Choice 3 High frustration tolerance (HFT) beliefs vs low frustration tolerance (LFT) beliefs

Ellis distinguishes between a high frustration tolerance (HFT) belief and a low frustration tolerance (LFT) belief. Let me outline and illustrate each one before you again choose which you would teach to your group of children. As I do so, remember that an HFT belief derives from a full preference and an LFT belief derives from a demand.

When you hold a full preference and desire, but do not demand, something then you are likely to hold a high frustration tolerance belief when your desire is not met. An HFT belief asserts that it is difficult to put up with not getting what you want, but it is tolerable and it is worth tolerating. An HFT belief is again therefore non-extreme in nature. On the other hand, when you hold a demand and your demand is not met you are likely to hold an LFT belief, where you assert that you cannot tolerate not getting what you demand. An LFT belief is therefore extreme in nature. Let me begin by outlining how you might teach children about HFT beliefs.

> Children, I have explained to you about the importance of keeping your desires flexible and not transforming them into rigid demands. If you do this, you will learn a third lesson:
>
> *When you don't get what you want and you don't demand that you have to get it, you will find this bearable although it may well be a struggle for you to bear it, especially when your strong desires have not been met. However, it will frequently be in your interests to bear this state of affairs.*
>
> When you hold an HFT belief you acknowledge that you will neither die nor disintegrate if your desires aren't met, nor will you lose the capacity for future happiness. Thus, if you want to go to university, but do not demand that you must do so, you acknowledge that not going would be difficult for you to bear, but that you could bear it and it would be in your interests to tolerate it. You can thus experience happiness in the future if you don't go to university.
>
> So, children, to sum up: when you want something, but do not demand that you have to get it, remind yourself that not getting what you want is bearable and worth bearing even if it is a struggle for you to put up with the deprivation.

Now, let me outline how you might teach children about LFT beliefs.

> Children, I have already told you about converting your strong desires into demands. When you do so and you don't get what you believe you must get, you will probably tell yourself this state of affairs is intolerable.
>
> When you hold an LFT belief you believe that if your demand, such as going to university, is not met then this is unbearable and you will never be happy again, or you will disintegrate or even die.

> So, children, to sum up: when you demand that you have to get what you want, you will also tend to believe that you can't bear it if your demand is not met.

You now know the difference between a high frustration tolerance (HFT) belief and a low frustration tolerance (LFT) belief. Once again, which of these two principles would you choose to teach to your group of children?

Choice 4 Acceptance beliefs vs depreciation beliefs

Ellis distinguishes between an acceptance belief and a depreciation belief. Let me outline and illustrate each one before you choose once again which you would teach to your group of children. As I do so, remember that an acceptance belief derives from a full preference and a depreciation belief derives from a demand.

When you hold a full preference and desire, but do not demand, something then you are likely to hold an acceptance belief when your desire is not met. An acceptance belief can refer to yourself (self-acceptance belief), to another person or group of people (other-acceptance belief) or to life conditions (life-acceptance belief). What these beliefs have in common is that they all assert the idea that you can rate aspects of self, others and life conditions and they all negate the idea that you can give a global, static rating to something as complex and organic as a person (self or others) or life. An acceptance belief, like a non-awfulizing belief or an HFT belief, is again therefore non-extreme in nature.

On the other hand, when you hold a demand and your demand is not met you are likely to hold a depreciation belief. A depreciation belief can also refer to yourself (self-depreciation belief), to another person or group of people (other-depreciation belief) or to life conditions (life-depreciation belief). What these beliefs have in common is that they all assert the idea that you can globally rate the self, others and life conditions as well as their different aspects. A depreciation belief, like an awfulizing belief or an LFT belief, is again therefore extreme in nature.

Let me begin by outlining how you might teach children about acceptance beliefs.

> Children, here is the fourth and final lesson that I want you to learn:
>
> *When you don't get what you want and you don't demand that*

> *you have to get it, if your thwarted desire is down to your own behaviour, you can rate your behaviour negatively without rating yourself negatively. Rather, you can accept yourself as a complex, unrateable, fallible human being whose behaviour is negative. If your thwarted desire is down to someone else's behaviour, you can accept him, for example, as a fallible human being who has acted badly. And if your thwarted desire is down to life conditions, you can rate these conditions negatively without depreciating the whole of life.*
>
> So, if you really want to go to university, but do not demand that you have to go, you will:
>
> 1 accept yourself, but dislike your behaviour if you were primarily responsible for your failure to get to university;
> 2 accept others, but dislike their behaviour if they were primarily responsible for your failure to get to university; and
> 3 accept life, but dislike the specific set of life circumstances that were primarily responsible for your failure to get to university.
>
> So, children, to sum up: when you want something, but do not demand that you have to get it, you will accept yourself, others or life for whoever or whatever is responsible for you not getting your desire met.

Now, let me outline how you might teach children about depreciation beliefs.

> Children, I have already told you about converting your strong desires into demands. When you do so and you don't get what you believe you must get, you will tend to depreciate yourself if you were responsible for not getting your demands met, depreciate others if they were responsible for you not getting what you believed you must get, or depreciate life if life conditions were responsible for not gratifying your demands.
>
> So, if you demand that you have to go to university, you will:
>
> 1 depreciate yourself if you were primarily responsible for your failure to get to university;
> 2 depreciate others if they were primarily responsible for your failure to get to university; and
> 3 depreciate life if a specific set of life circumstances were primarily responsible for your failure to get to university.

So, children, to sum up: when you make demands, you will depreciate yourself, others or life for whoever or whatever is responsible for you not getting your demands met.

You now know the difference between an acceptance belief and a depreciation belief. Finally, which of these two principles would you choose to teach to your group of children?

Now that I have outlined your four choices, my guess is that you would choose to teach your group of older children to hold full preferences and the non-awfulizing beliefs, high frustration tolerance beliefs and acceptance beliefs that are derived from them. Furthermore, you would also opt to encourage these children to refrain from making rigid demands of themselves, others and the world, and from holding awfulizing beliefs, low frustration tolerance beliefs and depreciation beliefs. Now if these healthy, rational beliefs are good enough for your tutees, aren't they also good enough for you? If you agree that they are, then you have made a very important first step along the path towards letting go of anxiety and depression. If, on reflection, you would rather think irrationally, then stop reading this book and instead read *How to Make Yourself Miserable* (Sheldon Press, 2001) which I wrote especially for people like you!!

Negative emotions: healthy vs unhealthy

During Rational Emotive Behaviour Therapy, while discussing my clients' disturbed reactions to negative events, events that very often appear in the guise of obstacles to these clients' cherished desires, there comes a stage when I ask my clients what they want to experience instead of their disturbed reactions. Very frequently, they respond to the effect that they want to feel a far less intense emotion or that they want not to care so much about not getting their cherished desires met. Taken at face value, these may seem reasonable goals, but when looked at more carefully they are problematic and raise important questions about what we are trying to do in psychotherapy. Is one of our prime objectives to help our clients to anaesthetize their negative feelings? Or is our goal to help them to reduce the intensity of their negative feelings? My response to both these questions is a resounding 'No!' In explaining why, let me outline REBT's view concerning negative emotions with special reference to anxiety and depression and their healthy counterparts.

As I have already discussed, REBT distinguishes between rational and irrational beliefs. When a person faces a negative activating event, she has a choice among three types of beliefs: rational beliefs, irrational beliefs and indifference beliefs. An indifference belief is where a person does not care one way or the other about the occurrence of an event. Thus, many of you would not care if Albion Rovers beat Queen's Park at football the next time they met in the Scottish third division. Your stance would be one of indifference to the outcome of this event. Now, indifference beliefs can be true or feigned. Your indifference towards the outcome of the Albion Rovers vs Queen's Park football match would probably truly reflect your attitude. However, if you demanded that you had to obtain promotion at work and you failed to do so, any attempt on your part to convince yourself and other people that you didn't care about your failure would constitute a feigned indifference belief, in that you would be trying to lie to yourself. Feigned indifference beliefs are conceptualized in REBT theory as ultimately unconstructive attempts to deal with the underlying presence of irrational beliefs.

If we therefore rule out indifference beliefs as a plausible way of responding to a negative activating event, we are left with a choice of holding a rational belief or an irrational belief towards this event. REBT theory states that in the face of negative events you have a choice of feeling bad but undisturbed about this event or of feeling bad and disturbed about it. Thus, when you hold a rational belief about a negative event you will experience a healthy negative emotion and when you hold an irrational belief about this same event you will experience an unhealthy negative emotion.

In the English language we do not have words that reliably and consensually discriminate between healthy negative emotions and unhealthy negative emotions, so the following list should be viewed as one person's attempt (i.e. mine) to discriminate linguistically between these different emotions. I see the following emotions as unhealthy and negative: anxiety, depression, guilt, shame, hurt, unhealthy anger, unhealthy jealousy and unhealthy envy. By contrast, I see the following emotions as their healthy and negative alternatives: concern, sadness, remorse, disappointment, sorrow, healthy anger, healthy jealousy and healthy envy. Thus, in this book I will encourage you to let go of anxiety in the face of threat and to feel concern instead, and to let go of depression in the face of loss or failure and to feel sad or disappointed instead.

In general, when you experience a healthy negative emotion (like sadness or concern), you do so, as discussed above, because you hold a rational belief about a negative event. In REBT theory this healthy negative emotion is known as an emotional consequence of a rational belief. There are two other consequences of rational beliefs: behavioural and thinking. Behavioural consequences of rational beliefs tend to be actions that are designed to change the negative event, if it can be changed, in ways that do not make life worse for the person in the longer run. They also involve actions that are designed to help the person to adjust constructively to this situation if it cannot be changed. Thinking consequences of rational beliefs are mostly realistic inferences about the present and future implications of the event. They are also problem-focused in that they help the person to think clearly about the behavioural options on offer that can help him to change the situation if it can be changed or to adjust to it constructively if it can't be changed.

Conversely, when you experience an unhealthy negative emotion (like anxiety or depression), you do so because you hold an irrational belief about a negative event. In REBT theory this unhealthy negative emotion is known as an emotional consequence of an irrational belief. As with rational beliefs, there are two other consequences of rational beliefs: behavioural and thinking. Behavioural consequences of irrational beliefs tend to be actions that are designed to change the negative event, if it can be changed, as quickly as possible. Unfortunately, these actions often result in the person making life worse for herself. They also involve actions that make it more difficult for the person to adjust constructively to this situation if it cannot be changed. Thinking consequences of irrational beliefs are mostly distorted inferences about the present and future implications of the event. They also encourage the person to take unconstructive, impulsive action because they interfere with the person's ability to think clearly about the behavioural options on offer, with respect to either changing the situation or adjusting constructively to it.

It is often assumed that unhealthy negative emotions are of greater intensity than healthy negative emotions. This may be true, but only at the very intense end of the continuum. For example, intense rage (unhealthy anger) is probably stronger than intense annoyance (healthy anger). However, the point here is that healthy anger can be intense. Therefore, it is psychologically healthy to experience strong healthy negative emotions whenever you face a negative event where one of your more important desires has not been met. This is such an important point that I am going to emphasize it and expand on it.

Whenever something negative happens that means that one of your more important desires has not been met, it is not healthy to have an attitude of indifference towards it and feel nothing. It is also not healthy to hold an irrational belief about it and feel an unhealthy negative emotion. The only healthy option is to hold a rational belief about the event and experience a healthy negative emotion. The greater the importance of your thwarted desire, the more intense will be your healthy negative emotion.

With respect to the issue of the intensity of a healthy negative emotion, I have already made the point that an intense healthy negative emotion is healthy by dint of its healthiness, even though it is intense. Remember that what determines the healthiness of a negative emotion is the rationality of the belief that underpins it. A major goal of REBT is to help people to feel healthily bad when they do not get their important desires met. Again, let me stress that the more important the thwarted desire is to the person, the more intense the healthy negative emotion will be. Thus, when a person comes to me for therapy because they are experiencing an unhealthy negative emotion about a thwarted desire that is very important to them, I will help that person to feel an appropriate strong healthy negative emotion instead. I will do so by helping that person to give up their irrational belief and instead hold a rational belief about having their important desire thwarted. I will not attempt to help the person by encouraging her to make her desire less important.

Summary

I have now laid the foundations of this book in this chapter. First and foremost, I discussed the central idea that you can choose to disturb yourself or un-disturb yourself about life's adversities by the beliefs that you choose to hold about these adversities. Second, I discussed the difference between healthy and unhealthy negative emotions and showed you that when it is clear that you are facing a real adversity, it is healthy to have a negative emotion about this adversity. I also pointed out that such negative emotions can be intense when the adversities that we face are highly negative. Please bear these points in mind when learning how to let go of anxiety (in the following chapter) and depression (in Chapter 3).

2

How to Let Go of Anxiety

Anxiety is one of the two most frequently experienced psychological problems, the other one being depression, which I will deal with in the following chapter. How then can you let go of this debilitating emotion? By understanding the dynamics of anxiety (i.e. how it works), and rigorously (but not rigidly) following a number of important psychological principles based on the psychology of concern, which is the healthy alternative to anxiety.

UNDERSTANDING THE DYNAMICS OF ANXIETY AND CONCERN

The following points show how anxiety and concern work.

- When you experience psychologically based anxiety (rather than anxiety that stems directly from physical causes) explicitly or implicitly, you think that you are facing some kind of psychological *threat*.
- Applying the REBT model which I outlined in Chapter 1, perception of threat *does not* cause anxiety. Rather, anxiety stems from a set of irrational beliefs about threat. Concern stems from a set of rational beliefs about threat. I will amplify these important points later in this chapter.
- Irrational beliefs can be specific or general. When they are specific, these irrational beliefs are held in specific situations. When they are general, they are held across relevant situations. General irrational beliefs (GiBs) lead to relevant specific irrational beliefs (SiBs). Thus, if you think that you must be approved by authority figures and you face a specific authority figure in a specific situation then you will, in all probability, hold a specific irrational belief in this situation (e.g. I must be approved by this authority figure in this situation).

  However, the presence of a specific irrational belief (say, about being approved by a specific authority figure in a specific situation) is not a reliable guide to whether or not you have a general irrational belief about being approved by authority figures in general. In order to know this, we need more information about how you react to authority figures across different situations.

Rational beliefs can also be general (GrBs) or specific (SrBs), and similar points to the ones just made also apply to these rational beliefs.

- When you hold a general irrational belief, you bring this to specific situations that could possibly embody the threatening theme of the irrational belief. When you do so, you tend to infer the presence of the threat in the absence of good corroborative evidence. For example, let's assume once again that you hold the following general irrational belief: 'I must be approved by authority figures.' If you are about to enter a specific situation where you will encounter a new authority figure whom you know nothing about and where you may be disapproved of (disapproval is the threatening theme here), then you will be much more likely to assume that this new authority figure will disapprove of you than you would if you held a general rational belief about being approved by authority figures. Holding the latter will lead you to infer the presence of threat only if it were clear that there was a very good chance that this specific authority figure would disapprove of you.

As I have just shown, bringing a general rational belief to specific situations that could embody the threatening theme would lead to inferences about the presence of threat when it was objectively clear that the threat was present.

It follows from this that a major way of letting go of anxiety is to hold a set of general rational beliefs about threat.

- In REBT, we often (but not always) encourage our clients to assume temporarily that their inferences are true. We do this to help our clients and ourselves identify the underlying irrational beliefs that are at the core of their psychological difficulties and see that they have a choice concerning whether to think irrationally or rationally about these inferences – in the case of anxiety and concern, inferences of threat.
- In order to make an informed choice on this issue, you need to understand the consequences of holding irrational and rational beliefs about threat. Table 1 lists these consequences.
- If you look at Table 1, you will see that most of the behavioural consequences and some of the thinking consequences of threat-related irrational beliefs are designed to rid yourself of anxiety as quickly as possible. In engaging in these behaviours and thoughts,

Irrational beliefs about threat	Rational beliefs about threat
Emotional consequences	***Emotional consequences***
Anxiety	Concern
Behavioural consequences	***Behavioural consequences***
Withdraw from the threat or seek safety if can't withdraw	Face the threat
Ward off or neutralize the threat	Deal constructively with the threat
Tranquillize feelings of anxiety	Experience feelings of concern
Seek reassurance about the threat	Think about threat without seeking reassurance
Overcompensate by facing an even bigger threat	Face and deal with the threat as it exists
Thinking consequences	***Thinking consequences***
When thinking about the threat, overestimate its negative features	When thinking about the threat, view it realistically
Underestimate ability to deal with the threat	Make realistic appraisal of ability to deal with threat
Have task-irrelevant thoughts *in situ*	Have task-relevant thoughts *in situ*
Exaggerate consequences of threat	Have realistic views of consequences of threat
Use cognitive distraction	Have constructive thoughts about facing and dealing with the threat
Have overcompensatory fantasies of dealing successfully with even bigger threats	Have constructive thoughts about facing and dealing with the threat as it exists

Table 1 Consequences of irrational and rational beliefs about threat

you keep yourself safe in the short term, but maintain your anxiety in the longer term because you neither face and deal effectively with threat when it exists, nor do you identify and challenge the irrational beliefs that underpin your anxiety. As you can see, the behavioural and thinking consequences of threat-related rational beliefs provide a much better bet for letting go of anxiety.

- Most of the thinking consequences of threat-related irrational beliefs lead you to think that you are under far more threat than is probably the case and that you are more vulnerable than is the case, whereas the thinking consequences of threat-related rational beliefs lead you to be more realistic in the appraisal of threat and in your ability to deal effectively with it.

- As the above two points show, when you think irrationally about threat you swing between trying to keep yourself safe and thinking that you are vulnerable and facing great threat. Neither of these positions actually helps you to deal effectively with threat in the long term. On the other hand, when you think rationally about threat you are motivated to face and deal effectively with threat, and feelings of concern help you to keep focused on doing so.
- Assuming that you have chosen to think rationally about threat rather than irrationally, you are now ready to work towards letting go of anxiety.

13 STEPS TO LETTING GO OF ANXIETY

In this section, I outline a number of steps that you need to take in order to let go of anxiety. Before I outline and describe these steps, I want to make two important points. First, in outlining these steps, I do not mean to imply that they are all essential and that if you miss any out, you will not make any progress in overcoming your anxiety. My view is that none of the steps is essential, but the more steps you follow the more likely it is that you will let go of anxiety. My second point concerns the order of the steps that I present. This order seems to me the most logical. It is not, however, meant to be set in stone and you may find that a different order works better for you. If so, fine. Experiment and see for yourself.

Step 1 Admit that you experience anxiety and that it is a problem for you

The first step to dealing with any problem is to admit that you have the problem. With anxiety, this involves two different steps: (1) admitting that you suffer from anxiety and (2) admitting that it is a problem for you. You may, for example, admit that you experience anxiety, but you may not see it as a problem for you. You may think that you need your anxiety in order to motivate yourself. If you think that anxiety is more beneficial than harmful to you, then keep a diary of when you feel anxious and review its effects. Also, would you encourage a group of children to feel anxious? Probably not. In which case, why not work to let go of it yourself?

Step 2 See that concern is a viable alternative to anxiety

However, if you are going to let go of anxiety then it is important that you see clearly that there is a specific, realistic and plausible alternative to anxiety. This alternative is known as concern. As you will see from Table 1, concern stems from rational beliefs about threat (whereas anxiety stems from irrational beliefs about threat) and it accompanies a set of behavioural and thinking consequences of threat-related rational beliefs that are far more constructive than the behavioural and thinking consequences of threat-related irrational beliefs that accompany anxiety.

Step 3 Accept yourself for feeling anxious

Once you have admitted that you suffer from anxiety and that it is a problem for you, it is important that you accept yourself for having these feelings and refrain from depreciating yourself for having an anxiety problem. Show yourself that you are not a weak person or a disturbed person for feeling anxious. Yes, anxiety may be a weakness or a disturbance in that it may interfere with the quality of your life, but this weakness or disturbance does not prove that you are a weak person or a disturbed person. It proves that you are an ordinary fallible human being who, along with millions of others, suffers from needless anxiety. Accepting yourself in this way will help you to focus on the task at hand, which is to work towards letting go of anxiety. Depreciating yourself for feeling anxious only gives you two problems for the price of one and certainly doesn't help you to deal constructively with your anxiety problem.

Step 4 List the situations in which you feel anxious and identify themes

The next step is for you to list specific situations in which you feel anxious, and once you have done this to look for common themes which span these situations. As you do this, you might find the following useful.

Common threats to self-worth include:

- failure;
- criticism;
- disapproval;
- rejection;
- loss of status.

Common threats which do not usually threaten your self-esteem include:

- loss of control;
- uncertainty;
- discomfort;
- loss of order;
- the experience of internal processes (e.g. unwanted thoughts, feelings, images and urges).

It is important to acknowledge that sometimes some of these threats may also be to your self-esteem.

Your next task is to look for common situational elements to your anxiety. For example, do you frequently feel anxious in particular recurring situations? If so, what are the aspects of these situations that you find most threatening?

Then, look for common interpersonal aspects to your anxiety. For example, do you frequently feel anxious with particular people or types of people? If so, who are these people (or types of people) and what is it about them that you find threatening?

Step 5 Identify your general threat-related irrational beliefs and their emotional, behavioural and thinking consequences

With the above information you should now be ready to identify your general threat-related irrational beliefs. What you do is to bring together the above identified themes (and relevant situational and/or interpersonal features) with the relevant irrational beliefs that I discussed in detail in Chapter 1. If you recall, these are as follows:

- rigid demands (e.g. musts, absolute shoulds, oughts, got to's, etc.);
- awfulizing beliefs (e.g. It's awful that . . . , It's terrible that . . . , It's the end of the world that . . . , etc.);

- low frustration tolerance (LFT) beliefs (e.g. I can't bear it, I can't stand it, It's intolerable, etc.);
- depreciation beliefs. There are three types of depreciation beliefs: self-depreciation beliefs (e.g. I am worthless, I am a bad person, I am inadequate, etc.); other-depreciation beliefs (e.g. You are worthless, You are a bad person, You are inadequate); and life-depreciation beliefs (e.g. Life is bad). All may be relevant to anxiety, but the most common are self-depreciation beliefs and life-depreciation beliefs.

When formulating general threat-related irrational beliefs, I suggest the following two principles:

Principle 1

If your anxiety is primarily ego-based, meaning that your anxiety is about threats to your self-esteem, then include the following components in formulating your general threat-related irrational belief:

- theme of threat (specifying any recurring situations and/or people);
- demanding belief + self-depreciation belief.

Here are a few examples, together with their emotional, behavioural and thinking consequences:

General threat-related irrational belief: ego-based	***Consequences of GiB***
I must not fail at important tasks. If I do it will mean that I am a failure.	– Anxiety on attempting tasks – Predicting failure when facing such tasks – Overestimating the negative consequences of failure – Avoiding attempting important tasks – Only attempting tasks that I can do

Bosses must not criticize my work. If they do, I am stupid.	– Anxiety in the presence of bosses – Predicting criticism from bosses whenever they see my work – Overestimating the negative consequences of bosses' criticism – Doing everything I can to make my work perfect and thus beyond criticism – Taking every opportunity to hide my work from my boss
Family members must not disapprove of me. If they do, it will prove that I am unlovable.	– Anxiety in the presence of family members – Predicting disapproval from family members whenever I see them – Overestimating the negative consequences of disapproval from family members – Doing everything I can to be approved by family members

Principle 2

If your anxiety is primarily non-ego-based, meaning that your anxiety is about threats other than to your self-esteem, then include the following components in formulating your general threat-related irrational belief:

- theme of threat (specifying any recurring situations and/or people);
- demanding belief + awfulizing belief or LFT belief.

Here are a few examples, together with their emotional, behavioural and thinking consequences:

General threat-related irrational belief: non-ego-based	*Consequences of GiB*
My breathing must be regular at all times and it will be awful if it isn't.	– Anxiety about facing any pressure in case breathing gets irregular – Predicting irregular breathing whenever under pressure – Overestimating the negative consequences of irregular breathing (e.g. heart attack) – Avoiding putting myself under pressure – Only attempting tasks during which I know I will be able to control my breathing
I must know that my loved ones are safe and I can't bear it if I don't know this.	– Anxiety in the presence of uncertainty about the whereabouts of my loved ones – Predicting that harm will come to my loved ones if I don't know that they are safe – Overestimating the extent of the harm as time unfolds, and this is reflected in ever grimmer harm befalling loved ones – Insisting that my loved ones call me to reassure me that they are safe – Telephoning my loved ones to reassure myself that they are safe

I must not lose the comforts of my lavish lifestyle and if I do it will be dreadful.	– An ongoing sense of anxiety whenever I think how comfortable my lifestyle is, since I am aware that I could easily lose it – Predicting threats to my lifestyle when none objectively exists – Overestimating the negative consequences of any disruption to my lifestyle – Doing everything I can to maintain my lifestyle

Step 6 Challenge your general threat-related irrational beliefs, then develop and rehearse an alternative set of general rational beliefs

In order to let go of anxiety, it is important that you operate according to a set of general rational beliefs about threat. In order to do this you need to weaken your conviction in your general threat-related irrational beliefs and develop and strengthen your conviction in an alternative set of general rational beliefs about threat.

I suggest that you re-read Chapter 1, particularly the material on pages 2–10 where I go over arguments why demands, awfulizing beliefs, LFT beliefs and depreciation beliefs are irrational, and why full preferences, non-awfulizing beliefs, HFT beliefs and acceptance beliefs are rational. Then you can apply similar arguments to your general irrational and rational beliefs about threat. In doing so I suggest that you use the following format:

1 State your general irrational belief.
2 Give reasons why your general irrational belief is irrational.
3 State the alternative general rational belief.
4 Give reasons why your general rational belief is rational.

Here is an example of how to do this.

The case of Angie

Here is how Angie used the four guidelines to help her develop a healthy general rational belief about threats to her self-esteem:

1 State your general irrational belief:

Bosses must not criticize my work. If they do, I am stupid.

2 Give reasons why your general irrational belief is irrational:

Sadly, there is no law of the universe that decrees that bosses must not criticize my work. I am just not immune from their criticism even though I would like to be. If I were, it would be impossible for bosses to criticize my work, which unfortunately is not the case.

Any criticism that my bosses make of my work cannot ever prove that I am stupid. For me to be stupid, this would have to be my identity and everything that I do would have to be stupid, which is obviously not the case. Also, even if my bosses' criticism means that the work that they criticize is bad, this does not prove that I am stupid, only that a part of me is (i.e. my work cannot define the whole of me). Thinking that my work can define me is an error of logic known as the part–whole error.

Also, as long as I hold this general irrational belief, then I will be anxious around my bosses and act and think in anxious ways consistent with this belief.

3 State the alternative general rational belief:

I would much prefer it if bosses did not criticize my work, but I am not immune from their criticism. If they do criticize my work, this does not mean that I am stupid even if my work is. It means that I am an ordinary fallible human being capable of good and bad work.

4 Give reasons why your general rational belief is rational:

It is true both that I would prefer my bosses not to criticize my work and that I'm not immune from their criticism. Also, any criticism they make of my work does prove that I am a fallible human being since this is my true nature, and even if I do work that is below standard, it does not mean that I have lost the ability to do good work. I am capable of both. My worth as a person can never truly be defined by the quality of my work or whether my bosses like my work or are critical of it.

If I develop and hold this general rational belief, then I will be concerned, but not anxious around my bosses and I will act and think in non-anxious ways consistent with this belief.

Follow the above four guidelines, review your arguments regularly and rehearse your general rational belief. As you develop greater conviction in your general rational belief about threat, you will find that you will increasingly bring it to situations where you previously overestimated the presence of threat and you will make much more realistic appraisals of threat, only seeing threat when it probably exists.

Step 7 Analyse specific episodes of anxiety

If you think about it, you experience anxiety in specific situations in which you consider that you are a facing some kind of threat and when you hold specific irrational beliefs about threat. As this is the case, you need a format in which to assess the important factors that are involved in your specific anxiety response as a prelude to learning to overcome your situationally based anxiety. I suggest the following framework, known as the 'situational ABC model'.

Situation

We do not react in a vacuum. Rather, we think, feel and act in specific situations. The term 'situation' in the 'situational ABC model' refers to a descriptive account of the actual event to which we respond emotionally and behaviourally.

Describe the situation in which you were anxious as objectively as possible.

A = Activating event

Within this specific situation, when you are anxious it is usually about some key or critical aspect of this situation which you perceive as a threat. This is known as the activating event.

Ask yourself the following: What aspect of the situation I have just described was I most anxious about or did I find most threatening? (Assume temporarily that your A is true. The best time to question the validity of A is when you are thinking rationally about it.)

B = Irrational belief

Remember that in REBT A does not cause your anxiety. Rather, your anxiety is primarily determined by the beliefs that you hold about A.

For a threat to your self-esteem (ego threat) write down your demanding belief and your associated self-depreciation belief. For other threats (non-ego threat), write down your demanding belief and either your awfulizing belief or your low frustration tolerance belief.

C = Consequences of the irrational beliefs at B about the activating event at A

When you hold a belief about an activating event at A, you will tend to experience an emotion, you will tend to act in a certain way and you will tend to think in certain ways. These three consequences of this AxB interaction are known as emotional, behavioural and thinking consequences respectively.

Identify your anxiety (emotional consequence), the way you acted or felt like acting while feeling anxious (behavioural consequences) and how you thought while feeling anxious (thinking consequences).

Let's now see how one person used the situational ABC model to analyse a specific episode of anxiety.

The case of Harry

Situation = Waiting for my wife to come home. She says that she will be home at 5.30 p.m. It is now 5.45 p.m.

A (Aspect of the situation that I was most anxious about) = Not knowing for certain that my wife is safe.

B (Irrational beliefs) = I must know for certain that my wife is safe. It is terrible not to know this.

C (Consequences of BxA)
Emotional (unhealthy negative) = Anxiety
Behavioural (unconstructive) = 1 Pacing up and down.
2 Keep on looking out of the window.
3 Looking up telephone numbers of local hospital casualty departments.
Thinking (unrealistic and skewed) = 1 Thinking that she has had a car crash.
2 Images of her funeral

(*and* believing that these thoughts were a reliable guide to what was happening and what would happen to my wife).

Step 8 Challenge your specific threat-related irrational beliefs, then develop and rehearse an alternative set of specific rational beliefs

Having accurately assessed the factors associated with your situationally based anxiety, you are now ready to challenge your specific threat-related irrational beliefs and to develop their specific rational alternatives. To do this you use similar guidelines to the ones that I outlined on page 24. Applying these guidelines to challenging specific beliefs we have:

1 State your specific irrational belief.
2 Give reasons why your specific irrational belief is irrational.
3 State the alternative specific rational belief.
4 Give reasons why your specific rational belief is rational.

Here is how Harry used the four guidelines to help develop alternative specific rational beliefs about his wife being late:

1 State your specific irrational belief:

I must know for certain that my wife is safe. It is terrible not to know this.

2 Give reasons why your specific irrational belief is irrational:

If there were a law of the universe that stated that I had to know for certain that my wife was safe on this occasion, then I would know this. Unfortunately, there is no law and as long as I demand that there is one, I will be anxious. Also, it is not terrible not to know for certain that my wife is safe since much worse things exist than my uncertainty, and as long as I believe it is I will be anxious and imagine all kinds of bad things happening to her.

3 State the alternative specific rational belief:

I would like to know for certain that my wife is safe, but I do not need to know that this is the case. It is uncomfortable not to know that she is safe, but it certainly isn't awful.

4 Give reasons why your specific rational belief is rational:

It is true that I would like to know that my wife is safe on this occasion and it is also true that I don't have to know this. Believing this will lead me to experience concern about her, but to keep my thoughts about what has happened to her in a realistic perspective. Yes, I can prove that it is uncomfortable not knowing that my wife is safe, but it is hardly terrible not to know this. Uncertainty does not inevitably mean that something bad has happened to her. In fact, when I take the terror out of my thinking, I can see that the probability is that she has been delayed.

Once you have followed these guidelines, rehearse your specific rational belief and then move on to the next step.

Step 9 Confront threat sensibly while rehearsing rational beliefs and while thinking realistically and acting healthily

This step is perhaps the most important one of all. After you have gained some experience of challenging your specific threat-related irrational belief and have spent some time rehearsing the specific alternative rational belief (as advised above), it is important for you to confront what you are afraid of. When you do this it is not only important that you rehearse your specific rational belief, but also that you act and think in ways that are consistent with this specific belief. The best way of determining constructive ways of acting and thinking is to re-do your situational ABC, this time based on holding a specific rational belief.

The case of Harry revisited

Here is how Harry re-did his ABC.

Situation = Waiting for my wife to come home. She says that she will be home at 5.30 p.m. It is now 5.45 p.m.

A = Not knowing for certain that my wife is safe.

B (Rational beliefs) = I would like to know for certain that my wife is safe, but I do not need to know this. It is uncomfortable not to know that she is safe, but it certainly isn't awful.

C = Emotional (healthy negative) = Concern

Behavioural (constructive) =
1. Continue to read my book.
2. Do not pace up and down, keep on looking out of the window or look up telephone numbers of local hospital casualty departments.

Thinking (realistic and balanced) =
1. Thinking that she has probably been delayed.
2. If I have thoughts that she has had a car crash or images of her funeral, I acknowledge that these are unlikely scenarios and allow these thoughts to go through my mind without trying to get rid of them or without acting on them.

How Harry confronted his threat

Once Harry had re-done his ABC, he waited for his wife to come home while sitting quietly reading a novel. He refrained from pacing up and down the room, from looking frequently out of the window and from checking the phone numbers of local casualty departments, actions that would have led him back to feeling anxious. He also reminded himself from time to time that the probability was that she was safe, and although he occasionally had thoughts of her having had a car crash and images of her funeral while he read, he allowed these thoughts to pass through his mind since he realized where they came from. Had he engaged with these thoughts and images, he would have again gone back to being anxious and strengthened his irrational belief in the process.

General comments about confronting threat

I want to make the following points about confronting threat.

- The best way to confront threat is when to do so is challenging, but not overwhelming, for you.
- It is useful to imagine confronting the threat in your mind before you do so in reality. When you do this, imagine that you are confronting the threat while rehearsing your specific rational belief and acting and thinking in ways that are consistent with this rational belief.
- When you imagine confronting threat, it is best to do so imagining that you will find it a struggle to hold on to your rational belief and related constructive behaviour and realistic thinking, a struggle where you succeed in the end, but a struggle nonetheless. If you imagine confronting threat with ease and that you masterfully hold on to your rational belief, etc., then you will not be gaining realistic practice for when you confront threat in reality.
- I say this because when you confront the threat in reality, you will in all probability struggle to hold on to your rational belief; you may well experience the urge to act in your usual unhealthy way and your initial thoughts may be unrealistic. If you accept that this will happen and that you need to persist in keeping your rational belief in the forefront of your mind, in acting in constructive but unaccustomed ways and in keeping your thoughts balanced and

realistic, then you will gain most from confronting threat in reality.

- Assume, in the first instance, that the threat that you are going to confront does in fact exist. Thus, if you are anxious about facing your boss's criticism and you have practised confronting this threat in your mind before doing so in reality, when you do so in reality assume that your boss will in fact criticize you. In this way, you will gain practice in thinking rationally and realistically and in behaving constructively even if the boss does not criticize your work. In order to let go of anxiety you need to learn two major principles. First, holding general rational beliefs will lead you to perceive threat accurately. Second, holding specific rational beliefs when threat does exist will help you to deal with the actual threat with due concern rather than with anxiety.

Step 10 How to deal with the thinking consequences of irrational beliefs

There is one important point about anxiety that you need to bear in mind when thinking about which threat to confront. Threats can occur at A in the situational ABC framework and they can also occur as a thinking consequence of an irrational belief about this same threat at A. Threats that are thinking consequences of irrational beliefs are usually much more exaggerated than threats that trigger irrational beliefs. Here are a few examples which will clarify what I mean:

Example 1

A (threat): My boss may criticize me.
B (irrational belief): My boss must not criticize me and it will be terrible if he does.
C (thinking consequence: new threat): I will be fired and never get another job again.

Example 2

A (threat): I am beginning to lose control over my breathing.
B (irrational belief): I must gain immediate control over my breathing and it will be awful if I don't.
C (thinking consequence: new threat): If I don't control my breathing I'll have a heart attack and die.

Example 3

A (threat): I may say something stupid at the party.
B (irrational belief): I must not say anything stupid at the party and if I do it proves that I am a stupid person.
C (thinking consequence): If I say something stupid everyone will laugh at me and I'll become a social outcast.

As these examples show, you start out with a negative threat at A and end up with a catastrophic threat at C because you hold an irrational belief at B about the original threat at A. Once you have made this connection between the original threat at A and the exaggerated thinking consequence at C via your irrational belief, and you have rehearsed this connection a number of times, you very quickly think of the exaggerated scenario whenever you think of the original threat. Applying this to the above examples:

1 Whenever the person thinks of his boss criticizing him, he very quickly thinks that this will lead to him losing his job and being unemployable.
2 Whenever the person begins to lose control of her breathing, she thinks that this will lead to her having a heart attack.
3 Whenever the person thinks that he may say something stupid at a party, he thinks that others present will laugh at him and this will lead to him becoming a social outcast.

So far, I have urged you to assume temporarily that the threat that you predict at A is real so that you can identify, challenge and change your irrational belief at B. The question that you probably have at this time is: How can I best deal with the thinking consequences of my irrational beliefs? Let me begin by outlining your options and consider the issues that emerge from each of these options.

Option 1 Go back to challenge your irrational belief

When you think that you are facing a very exaggerated threat, understand that this is evidence that you are operating on an irrational belief about a prior less exaggerated threat. Use this as a cue to go back to challenge this irrational belief.

Option 2 Let the thoughts be and allow them to pass through your mind

When you think that you are facing a highly exaggerated threat and you have challenged the irrational belief about the prior less exaggerated threat (see above), understand that these exaggerated thoughts are vestiges of this irrational belief and that they will eventually go if you do not engage with them or act on them. Rather, treat them as trains passing you by as you stand on a platform. In other words, allow these thoughts to come into your mind and go out the other side without engaging with them in thought or in deed.

Option 3 Question the realism of the thinking consequence

When you think that you are facing a very exaggerated threat, question how realistic it is, given the actual situation you are in. Thus, if you say something stupid at a party, ask yourself how likely it is that everyone there will laugh at you and how likely it is that you will be a social outcast as a result. How would you respond if a close friend told you that if she said something stupid she thought that she would face such exaggerated consequences? What is a more realistic conclusion instead? Such a conclusion is usually more balanced. In this case, a more realistic balanced conclusion would be something like, 'If I say something stupid at the party, some people may laugh at me, some may feel for me and others may not notice. Some may even find what I say amusing. Whatever happens, it is highly unlikely that I will be a social outcast.'

It is generally easier to implement Option 3 once you have carried out Option 1.

In Step 7, I showed you how to analyse a specific example of your anxiety. In doing so I encouraged you to assume temporarily that your A (the aspect of the situation about which you were most anxious) was true. I did this because this is the best way to identify your irrational belief that we in REBT argue is at the very core of your anxiety. In Step 7, I argued that the best time to question the validity of your A is when you are thinking rationally about it. Thus, after you have challenged your irrational belief about the A (Option 1), use the questions that I have outlined in this section to question the validity of your A (Option 3).

Option 4 Conduct behavioural experiments

When you are facing a very exaggerated threat it is important to test out in reality whether the threat is real or not. Now, I fully appreciate that it 'feels' real, in the sense that when you have made yourself anxious the major thinking consequence of your irrational belief is an exaggerated threat that you generally think will occur. However, in anxiety it is important that you learn that what 'feels' real or seems real may well be the unrealistic exaggerated thinking consequences of an irrational belief. As I have pointed out in Option

1, one way of distancing yourself from the very 'real' exaggerated threat is to stand back and understand that this is a product of your irrational belief rather than an accurate reflection of what is going on. If you have challenged your irrational belief first, you will find this easier to do.

Sometimes this is not enough and you need to test out in reality whether the exaggerated threat is real or not. This involves carrying out behavioural experiments where you confront the situation in reality without the use of any safety-seeking behaviours or thoughts. For example, if you think that everyone will laugh at you and you will become a social outcast if you say something stupid at a party, then one way of testing this is to say something stupid and see what happens. Experience can be a very powerful teacher, and if you do this a reasonable number of times you will learn the powerful lesson that your exaggerated thinking is a product of your irrational thinking and not a reliable guide to reality because it 'feels' or seems real.

Behavioural experiments are an integral part of the treatment of panic disorder. We now know that at the core of a panic attack is what some theorists call a catastrophic misinterpretation of threat. This is virtually the same as a thinking consequence of an irrational belief that is highly exaggerated in nature. For example, frequently at the core of a panic attack is the thought that the person is having a heart attack. Unless the person understands the dynamics of panic she will do anything to avoid having a heart attack: avoid doing certain activities, avoid certain places where she has had such catastrophic thoughts before and engage in subtle behaviours that keep her safe, at least in her mind, from overtaxing her heart. All these ways of responding are based on the person's implicit conviction that her thought, 'I will have a heart attack', accurately reflects reality. Actually, this thought is far more likely to be a grossly exaggerated thinking consequence of a prior irrational belief, e.g. 'I must calm down now and if I don't it will be terrible → and I will have a heart attack if I don't.' In this example, by demanding that she calms down, the person actually makes herself more anxious, and believing that it is terrible to experience ongoing and rising anxiety leads the person easily to misinterpret heightened anxiety as evidence of having a heart attack.

Once this person has challenged her irrational belief, she still has to disprove her inference that her anxiety symptoms are evidence that she will imminently have a heart attack rather than evidence of anxiety. The best way for her to do this is to stay in the situation, do avoided activities associated with the idea of having a heart attack and resist engaging in subtle behaviours that she constructed to keep herself safe. If you suffer from panic disorder, you may need additional help along the lines that I have briefly outlined; ask your GP to refer you to a therapist or counsellor who practises Rational Emotive Behaviour Therapy (REBT) or cognitive-behaviour therapy (CBT).

Option 5 Assume the thinking consequence will occur and think rationally about it

The final way of dealing with an exaggerated thinking consequence of an irrational belief is to assume temporarily that it will happen and to dispute your irrational belief about that consequence.

Since this may seem rather confusing, let me put it in diagrammatic form and provide an example. This example is the one I first introduced on page 32.

A (original threat): I may say something stupid at the party.
B (irrational belief): I must not say anything stupid at the party and if I do it proves that I am a stupid person.
C (thinking consequence): If I say something stupid everyone will laugh at me and I'll become a social outcast.

↓

A (new threat): Everyone will laugh at me and I will become a social outcast.
B (irrational belief): That would be dreadful. I couldn't tolerate that.

As this diagram shows, the person's exaggerated thinking consequence of his original irrational belief then becomes the new activating event on which he focused and on which he holds another irrational belief. Using Option 5, the person would endeavour to show himself that if everybody did laugh at him and he did become a social outcast, then that would be a very bad situation indeed, but it still wouldn't be terrible. Terrible means that nothing good could come out of this situation, and the person would show himself that this would *not* be the case. He could, for example, endeavour to meet a new group of friends, people who would be tolerant of human stupidity, and if this happened, he would actually be in a better situation than he was before. He would also show himself that it would certainly be difficult to tolerate being a social outcast, but that it is tolerable (he would neither die nor forfeit his capacity to be happy) and that it would be worth tolerating in that he could, as shown above, endeavour to meet a more tolerant group of friends.

If the person was successful at disputing his irrational belief about being laughed at and becoming a social outcast, then he would lose his anxiety about this admittedly highly aversive event, and in doing so he would be able to see that it is a grossly exaggerated event and one that is very unlikely to occur.

Thinking rationally about highly aversive events that are in reality unlikely to occur (although always possible) is a great antidote to anxiety. However, as you are probably thinking, it is difficult to do. Yet it is possible, and if you are prepared to work hard at thinking rationally you may well be able to think rationally even about the highly aversive events.

The founder of REBT, Albert Ellis, did this in overcoming his fear of flying. When on a particularly bumpy flight in a small plane in a bad storm, he overcame his fear of flying by vigorously convincing himself of the following: 'If I die tonight on this plane, I die. Too bad! There is no reason why I must not die in this fashion.' Now I am fully aware that not everyone reading this book will be able to think rationally about their own demise and about other highly aversive life events. However, if you don't attempt this at all, you certainly won't succeed. So assume temporarily that a highly aversive event that you created through your irrational belief about the original threat will occur, and work to think rationally about this. If you succeed you will make yourself far less vulnerable to anxiety and you will then be able to see that highly aversive events are unlikely to occur.

In this section, I have outlined five ways of dealing with the thinking consequences of your irrational beliefs. Become familiar with each of these options and use whichever method or methods (since you can use more than one) is/are most appropriate.

Step 11 Commit yourself to confront threat on a regular basis and generalize your learning

So far I have outlined a number of important ingredients to letting go of anxiety. I have argued that it is important that you identify and challenge both your general and specific threat-related irrational beliefs and that you develop increasing conviction in your alternative rational beliefs. You can best do this by confronting threat in imagination and particularly in reality, while rehearsing your rational beliefs and while acting and thinking in ways that are consistent with these rational beliefs.

While doing this you need to understand that you may experience the urge to go back to well-established behavioural reactions to threat that are largely designed to keep you safe in the moment. Acting on these urges will lead you to feel safe in the short term, but will perpetuate your anxiety in the longer term because doing so does not give you opportunities to think rationally about threat in the presence of that threat. Thus, it is important for you to refrain from acting on these urges to seek immediate safety.

I also argued that you need to understand how holding irrational beliefs about threat can lead you very quickly to think of far more aversive threats, and I outlined five approaches to responding constructively to these exaggerated thinking consequences of irrational beliefs.

If you follow these guidelines and apply them in a *repeated* and *consistent* manner to each of the threats about which you tend to make yourself anxious, then you will assuredly make progress in letting go of anxiety.

I have stressed the terms 'repeated' and 'consistent' here for good reason. First, just facing a threat once will not help you much, even though you are rehearsing a rational belief and acting and thinking in ways that are consistent with that belief. You need to do this a good number of times before your feelings change. I liken psychological change to a greyhound race with four dogs named Belief, Behaviour, Thinking and Emotion. When the trap door goes up, all the dogs apart from Emotion leave their traps and start running round the track; Emotion is very late to leave but soon catches up with the other dogs. Thus, do not expect to feel concerned rather than anxious until you have exercised your rational beliefs and associated constructive behaviour and realistic thinking on many occasions. For example, when I was a young boy I was badly bitten by an Alsatian dog and developed a fear of this breed. It was only when I approached them (constructive behaviour) while believing that I could tolerate doing so (rational belief) and realizing that they were unlikely to attack me (realistic thinking), and *did so repeatedly*, that I let go of my anxiety of Alsatian dogs.

Another important ingredient in letting go of anxiety is to generalize your learning across situations. Earlier in this chapter, I encouraged you to identify the themes that underpin events about which you make yourself anxious (e.g. rejection, disapproval, losing control). Once you have confronted being criticized in one situation (while rehearsing a rational belief and acting and thinking in ways that are consistent with this belief), then seek out other situations in which you think you may be criticized and practise the healthy belief–behaviour–thinking process while concentrating on being criticized. Even if you are not criticized in any given situation, you have gained valuable practice at handling such criticism in a healthy fashion.

Step 12 Deal with obstacles to making progress

You may have gained the impression that letting go of anxiety is a relatively straightforward process with no hitches. However, nothing could be further from the truth, and you will probably either wittingly or unwittingly prevent yourself from letting go of your anxiety in a number of ways. Why will you probably do this? Simply because you are human, and humans frequently get in their own way while carrying out personal change programmes. I will now outline ways of overcoming some of the common obstacles to making progress in dealing with anxiety.

Overcoming Obstacle 1 Accept yourself for creating obstacles to progress

Once you have recognized that you have been stopping yourself in some way from doing what you need to do to let go of your anxiety, then it is important that you accept yourself as a fallible human being who is not immune from self-defeat. If you depreciate yourself for creating obstacles to progress, you are in fact demanding that you absolutely should not do what is natural for humans to do: stop themselves in some way from continuing to work productively to let go of anxiety. Sadly, all the demanding in the world that you must not defeat yourself will not make you stop doing so, and indeed, demanding that you must not create an obstacle to progress in the first place only serves to create a second, more pernicious obstacle in the second place. This is because when you are demanding that you must not defeat yourself, you are not only preventing yourself from understanding how you are stopping yourself from letting go of anxiety and thereby from dealing effectively with this obstacle, you are creating a second emotional problem, e.g. depression, shame or anger at yourself for 'falling off the wagon'. If you want to make yourself miserable this is a good tactic, but if you sincerely wish to let go of anxiety, it is important that you accept yourself unconditionally as a person who has done the wrong thing, i.e. prevented yourself from going forward. Doing this will help you get back on track.

Overcoming Obstacle 2 Learning that understanding is not enough

Once you have learned about and understood the dynamics of anxiety and the steps you need to take to let go of this debilitating emotion, you may think that such understanding is sufficient for you to achieve this goal. It is most decidedly not. Imagine you read a book about swimming. Is that all you would need to do in order to learn to swim? Of course not! Well, the same is true with learning to let go of anxiety. Understanding is an important prelude to taking effective action, to be sure, but it is only that, a prelude. The key to letting go of anxiety, as I have reiterated throughout this chapter, is to repeatedly confront threat while rehearsing rational beliefs and acting and thinking in ways that are consistent with these rational beliefs. Learning that this is what you need to do is important, but won't, on its own, help you. *Acting* on this principle will.

Overcoming Obstacle 3 'Feel the fear and do it anyway'

Feel the Fear and Do It Anyway is the title of a best-selling book by Susan Jeffers (Arrow, 1991). While I do not agree with everything that Susan says in the book, I fully endorse the principle that is enshrined in the book's title. So many people think that they cannot do anything constructive to help themselves when they are feeling anxious. They believe that their anxiety has to completely subside or be significantly reduced before they confront their threat. I learned many years ago, well before I became a psychologist, that this wasn't true. I have a stammer, and in my teens I was very anxious about speaking up in case I stammered. Believing in the 'Only do it when you don't feel the fear' principle, I would either wait until I was relaxed before speaking in public or I would use subtle tricks to avoid stammering and thus not feel anxious. However, this only served to perpetuate my fear of stammering. It was only when I determined to speak up in public and practised the healthy belief 'If I stammer, I stammer. Too bad! It's unfortunate if I do, but hardly the end of the world' that I began my path to letting go of my anxiety about stammering. But, and this is the point, in the beginning as I spoke up I was still anxious about stammering because my new rational belief hadn't 'kicked in', and wouldn't do so until I had practised it many times while rehearsing my rational belief and acting and thinking in ways that were consistent with it. Please note the paradox: in order to let go of anxiety I had to take action while I was anxious! I had to feel the fear and speak up anyway. So take Susan Jeffers' advice and don't wait until you are relatively anxiety-free before taking constructive action. Feel the fear and do it anyway!

Overcoming Obstacle 4 Learn that anxiety is rarely dangerous

In order to implement the 'Feel the fear and do it anyway' principle, you also need to learn that, in the vast majority of cases, anxiety is not dangerous. It can be very uncomfortable, to be sure, but dangerous? Rarely. Now, if at the core of your anxiety problem is a dire need for certainty, you will have made yourself anxious about my last statement. Why? Because a major consequence of a dire need for certainty is a personalizing of threat (i.e. thinking that one is at risk when others are not). Thus, when I write that anxiety can be dangerous but that this is rare, you think that it is dangerous for you because you cannot convince yourself for certain that it is not. With respect to things that you find threatening, when you believe that you must be sure that you are not under threat and you cannot convince yourself that you have such immunity, then you think that the threat applies to you even if objectively the risk is very slight. In order to deal with this situation you need to develop a healthy belief, namely that while certainty of immunity would be very nice, you definitely do not need such certainty. If you believe this when you face such uncertainty, which you will in many circumstances, you will recognize that it is very possible for you to be uncertain and in all probability safe from threat when objectively the threat is remote. Once you accept all of this you are ready to learn the circumstances where anxiety may be dangerous. These apply when your anxiety is sudden and very intense and your heart is very diseased, and even then it is far from inevitable that anxiety is dangerous.

Overcoming Obstacle 5 Go against the strong urge to feel safe in the short term

When you decide to face up to your fears and take action even though you are anxious, you may still short-circuit your progress by going along with your strong urge to feel safe in the short term. So, you may begin by feeling the fear and doing it anyway, but as you do you will still experience strong urges to go for a sense of immediate safety. Thus, you may act and think in ways that are designed to give you this immediate sense. These safety-seeking manoeuvres are quite natural and it is easy for you to adopt them unless you have a good reason not to. If you want to let go of your anxiety, there is a good reason not to, since when you implement such manoeuvres you deprive yourself of the opportunity of confronting threat while rehearsing rational beliefs and acting and thinking in ways that are consistent with these beliefs. So resist the urge to implement behavioural and thinking safety-seeking manoeuvres and instead resolve to act in ways that help you to confront the threat while rehearsing your rational beliefs. Here is an example of what I mean with respect to dropping a behavioural safety-seeking manoeuvre. Imagine that you are holding on to a supermarket trolley for dear life in case you faint (which you evaluate as terrible). Let go of the trolley and see what happens. You probably won't faint, but if you do, you have the opportunity to take the horror out of this experience and see how people actually respond to you as opposed to how you fear they may respond.

Overcoming Obstacle 6 Surrender your need for a guarantee and to be in control

In the section on learning that anxiety is in all probability a painful but benign experience, I discussed the dire need for certainty of immunity. The need for certainty applies more widely and is one of two rigid beliefs that account for much anxiety in the first place and explain why people don't succeed in letting go of anxiety in the second place. The other rigid belief is the dire need for control, and in particular self-control. I will discuss both here.

If you believe that you must have a guarantee that the steps that I have outlined in this chapter must work before you try them, then you won't try them, or if you do you will be anxious about the outcome of your efforts. Both stances would get in the way of you letting go of anxiety. You need to give up the idea that you must know that this self-help programme has to work if you use it and instead go along with the probability that you will benefit from it, especially if you implement the steps in a non-perfectionistic manner.

When you are anxious you are by definition not in as much control as you would like to be. Anxiety can be expressed in a variety of bodily ways. For example, you may sweat or your hands may shake. The best way to deal with these symptoms is to let them be. Acknowledge that they are uncomfortable, accept that they may be visible, but don't demand that you must bring them under your control, for when you make such a demand you usually mean that you must control such symptoms quickly. The effect of this demand is to increase your anxiety and its associated symptoms. When you demand to be in control of your bodily responses and you begin to lose control of them, you create thoughts and images (i.e. thinking consequences) where you lose complete control of yourself. Rather than expose yourself to this you will avoid situations where loss of control is possible. Since you are not going to let go of anxiety unless you develop a healthy attitude towards it, this poses a significant obstacle to your progress. Developing and practising a healthy attitude to the loss of control implicit in experiencing anxiety will help you to appreciate that this loss of control will not inevitably lead you to being totally out of control. An example of this rational belief is as follows: 'I would like to be able to stop sweating immediately, but I do not have to do this. If I sweat, I sweat. This is uncomfortable, but hardly the end of the world. If others notice and think that there is something wrong with me, they are wrong. I am a fallible human being who sweats when he is anxious. Too bad! This hardly makes me a weirdo.' Practising such beliefs will help you to confront both your feelings of anxiety and the situations in which you experience them.

Step 13 Develop and rehearse a non-anxious world view

As I explained in my book *How to Make Yourself Miserable* (Sheldon Press, 2001), people develop views of the world as it relates to them that make it more or less likely that they will experience unhealthy negative emotions. The world views that render you vulnerable to anxiety do so primarily because they make you oversensitive to the presence of threat about which you hold anxiety-related irrational beliefs. I have already discussed the importance of developing rational alternatives to these irrational beliefs at both the general and the specific level. In this final section, I discuss the importance of developing realistic views of the world that will help you to let go of anxiety. I will present an illustrative list of such world views, rather than an exhaustive one, to help you to develop your own. What I will do is to first describe a world view that renders you vulnerable to anxiety and then give its healthy alternative. You will see that the latter is characterized by its complexity and non-extreme nature, whereas in the former, aspects of the world that relate to threat are portrayed as unidimensional and extreme.

Views of the world that render you vulnerable to anxiety	**Views of the world that help you to let go of anxiety**
The world is a dangerous place.	The world is a place where danger exists, but where there is much safety.
Uncertainty is dangerous. Knowing in all probability that I am safe is not good enough.	Uncertainty can indicate the presence of threat, but more often than not it is associated with the absence of threat, a sign that I am safe from threat. Probability of safety is all I have and is good enough for me.
Not being in control is dangerous. Either I am in control or I am out of control.	Not being in control is unpleasant, but is rarely dangerous. Just because I am not in complete control certainly does not mean that I am out of control.
People cannot be trusted.	People vary enormously along a continuum of trustworthiness. My best stance is to trust someone unless I have evidence to the contrary. If I am let down that is very unfortunate, but hardly terrible, and won't unduly affect my stance towards the next person I meet.

If you hold rational beliefs that are consistent with the views of the world listed on the right-hand side of the above table and if you act and think in ways that are, in turn, consistent with these rational beliefs, then doing all this will help you to let go of anxiety.

HOW PHIL LET GO OF ANXIETY

In this closing section, I will tell the story of Phil, who used the principles in this book to help himself let go of anxiety. To preserve his confidentiality, I have changed any identifying details. Phil was a client of mine and thus used the principles with my counselling help. However, he put into practice outside of counselling sessions what he learned within them, and thus was practising self-help very early in the counselling process.

Phil experienced a lot of anxiety at work that mostly centred on how others evaluated his performance. He was a college lecturer who was referred to me because he felt he couldn't cope with the formal evaluation procedures that were introduced by his college. Here is how Phil progressed through the 13 steps that I described above.

Steps 1 and 3 Phil admits that he experienced anxiety and that it was a problem for him, and accepts himself for feeling anxious

Phil initially found it difficult to admit to himself and to me that he was anxious. At first, he would only use the term 'stress' and put the blame on his college for causing his stress by the formal performance evaluations that it had introduced. However, it transpired that Phil felt ashamed of his anxiety problem and his feelings of shame led him to deny feeling anxious. I helped him to see that he was an ordinary person with a problem and not the defective person that he thought he was for feeling anxious. Once he began to accept himself in this way, Phil began to admit to himself and to me the extent of his anxiety about being evaluated negatively, not only at work but in some social situations as well.

Step 2 Phil sees that concern is a viable alternative to anxiety

When I asked Phil what he wanted to achieve from counselling he said that he wanted to be 'cool' at work and when interacting socially with his academic colleagues. On further exploration, it transpired that for Phil 'cool' meant being relaxed and confident in the face of negative judgment. When I helped him to see that not liking being judged in negative ways was a healthy stance to take, and that to be concerned, but not anxious, about such judgment was a healthy feeling response to such a threat, Phil saw that such feelings of concern were a legitimate and viable alternative to being 'cool' and, of course, to feeling anxious when one thinks that one is going to be viewed in a negative light. I also helped Phil to see that, as he did this, he might discover that he was overestimating the extent to which he was being judged negatively by his colleagues and students and that, when he was more rational about being judged, he would be able to see the presence or absence of this threat more clearly.

Step 4 Phil lists the situations in which he felt anxious and identifies themes

Phil felt anxious in the following situations:

- lecturing in front of large groups of students (but not in small seminar settings);
- speaking at large academic meetings;
- presenting a paper at large conferences;
- interacting with academic colleagues at parties and cocktail parties.

In considering these situations with me, Phil came to realize that the following were important themes in his anxiety:

- being seen to be 'uncool' by his students;
- being judged as an academic fraud by his academic colleagues.

Step 5 Phil identifies his general threat-related irrational beliefs and their emotional, behavioural and thinking consequences

It was clear to both of us that Phil's anxiety was about threats to his self-esteem. Consequently, his general threat-related irrational beliefs and their emotional, behavioural and thinking consequences were as follows:

Phil's general threat-related irrational belief: ego-based	***Consequences of GiB***
I must not be seen to be 'abnormal' by my students and if I am this proves that I am defective.	– Being very anxious before giving lectures and taking prescribed beta-blockers to cope with and hide this anxiety – Predicting that I will get very anxious when lecturing – Thinking that students will notice me being anxious and think that I am 'abnormal' – Thinking that I will get a reputation on campus as a 'basket-case' – Cancelling lectures if anxiety is too great and blaming cancellations on a 'virus'
I must not be seen to be a fraud by my academic colleagues and if I am they are right and this proves that I am worthless.	– Feeling anxious in the presence of my academic colleagues in case they ask me about my research and feeling anxious thinking about such scenarios – Predicting that if I talk on academic subjects with my colleagues I will say mundane or stupid things – Predicting that my colleagues are bound to think I am a fraud if they hear me speak on academic topics – Thinking that I will get a national reputation in my academic field as a fraud – Avoiding speaking on academic topics with my colleagues as much as possible, and if I cannot avoid doing so, taking a beta-blocker or alcohol to calm down first

	– Getting junior colleagues to give academic papers at conferences on the pretext that I am helping their careers by doing so – If I have to give a formal academic paper in front of my peers and I cannot get out of it, I over-prepare and rehearse the paper far too many times

Step 6 Phil challenges his general threat-related irrational beliefs, then develops and rehearses an alternative set of general rational beliefs

Phil used the following guidelines to challenge his two general threat-related irrational beliefs and replace them with two alternative rational beliefs.

1 State your general irrational belief.
2 Give reasons why your general irrational belief is irrational.
3 State the alternative general rational belief.
4 Give reasons why your general rational belief is rational.

I will just present here the work that Phil did on the following GiB: 'I must not be seen to be "abnormal" by my students and if I am this proves that I am defective.'

1 State your general threat-related irrational belief:

I must not be seen to be 'abnormal' by my students and if I am this proves that I am defective.

2 Give reasons why your general irrational belief is irrational:

While it would be highly desirable for my students not to think of me as abnormal, I am not immune from this happening. If I was it couldn't happen, no matter how strangely I behaved in the lecture hall. As long as I operate according to this rigid belief, I will engage in all kinds of self-defeating behaviours such as avoiding giving lectures and taking drugs to get through them. If I continue like this I'll be hooked on taking these drugs for ever and I really don't want that. Also, holding this rigid belief leads me to think of threat all the time and probably leads me to overestimate how poorly I will come across in lectures and how badly my students will view me. Even if they do think I'm abnormal, they are wrong. I am an ordinary human being with an anxiety problem, like millions of people including a fair few of my students. If I can accept myself as such, then I will be able to concentrate on what I am teaching rather than on how I am coming across while I am teaching.

3 State the alternative general rational belief:

I really don't want to be seen to be 'abnormal' by my students, but I am not immune from this happening. If it does happen this would definitely not prove that I am defective. It only proves that I am an ordinary human being with a problem and also that these students were highly judgmental in their opinion of me.

4 Give reasons why your general rational belief is rational:

It is true that I really don't want to be seen to be 'abnormal' by my students, but it is also true that I am not immune from this happening. The fact that this can happen proves my lack of immunity. If it does happen then I can prove that I am an ordinary human being with a problem and not defective. If I were defective then everything about me would be defective, and this is hardly true. I am an ordinary human being and I have a problem. My rational belief indicates that this problem does not convert me from being ordinary to being defective. My rational belief also indicates that if my students judge me to be 'abnormal' for getting anxious in class, for example, this proves that they are being highly judgmental of me on this point and that I do not warrant such a rating of my personhood.

If I operate according to this flexible and non-extreme general rational belief, then I will engage in a set of constructive behaviours. I would face up to the possibility of lecturing while being anxious, without taking beta-blockers. If I accept being anxious without liking it, I will persist until I make myself feel healthily concerned, but not anxious, about the possibility of being judged negatively by my students.

Also, holding this rational belief will lead me to see the threat of being judged more realistically. I will see that if I show my anxiety while lecturing, then some students may well think that I am abnormal, others will view me as an ordinary person with an anxiety problem, yet others will think that I am brave for continuing to lecture despite being anxious, and a further group will experience compassion for me, while some students may not even notice that I am anxious. All this will allow me again to concentrate on what I am teaching rather than on how I am coming across while I am teaching.

Phil reviewed the above arguments regularly, and as he did so he rehearsed his general rational belief. As he came to really believe that he would be an ordinary person with a problem and not defective if his students considered him to be abnormal and didn't have to have a good opinion of him, he created less threat in his mind when he came to give lectures. He began to be more objective about students' opinions about him and generally considered that their views were benign unless it was clear that they were malicious.

He made similar progress on his other general threat-related irrational belief and really began to believe that it would be nice if his academic colleagues did not see him as a fraud, but that he was not immune from them doing so, in the same way as he was not immune from his students considering him to be abnormal. Furthermore, he really began to see that if any of his academic colleagues did see him as a fraud, then this neither made him a fraud nor proved their view that he was worthless. His worth remains the same no matter what his colleagues think of him, although he would much prefer it if they had a favourable opinion of him as an academic. Reviewing the arguments in support of this general rational belief and those against his general irrational belief, and also rehearsing the former, helped Phil to be more objective of how much threat he was under when he spoke about academic issues with his peers. He saw that his general irrational belief meant that he was viewing such discussions through threat-coloured glasses. Consequently, he became more open-minded about the likelihood of them being critical of his views and resolved to test this out later in therapy.

Step 7 Phil analyses specific episodes of anxiety

Phil used the situational ABC framework described earlier in this chapter to deal with a number of specific episodes of anxiety about lecturing in front of his students and of discussing academic issues with his colleagues. Here is an ABC that Phil did of a specific episode of the latter anxiety.

Situation

I am going to a drinks party attended by a number of my academic colleagues.

A = Activating event

I am most anxious about others questioning my academic credibility if I say something mundane about my research.

Note that, as suggested on page 26, Phil assumed temporarily that his inference at A was true. He did this so he could go on to identify his irrational belief that was at the root of his anxiety.

B = Irrational belief

Others at the party must not question my academic credibility if I say something mundane about my research, and if they do I am worthless.

C = Consequences of the irrational beliefs at B about the activating event at A

Emotional C = Anxiety

Behavioural C = Overpreparing what I am going to say if the topic of my research comes up.
Resolving to change the subject if the topic of my research comes up.
Plotting my escape if I say something mundane.

Thinking C = Thinking that my colleagues will think I am a fraud if I don't sparkle academically.
Thinking that my reputation will be more widely damaged if I say something mundane about my research.

Step 8 Phil challenges his specific threat-related irrational beliefs, then develops and rehearses an alternative set of specific rational beliefs

Phil used the following guidelines to challenge his specific threat-related irrational belief and replace it with an alternative specific rational belief.

1 State your specific irrational belief.
2 Give reasons why your specific irrational belief is irrational.
3 State the alternative specific rational belief.
4 Give reasons why your specific rational belief is rational.

1 State your specific threat-related irrational belief:

Others at the party must not question my academic credibility if I say something mundane about my research, and if they do I am worthless.

2 Give reasons why this specific irrational belief is irrational:

While it would be highly desirable for my colleagues not to question my academic credibility if I say something mundane about my research at the party, there is no law that dictates that they must not do so. They may do so and if they do it does not prove that I am worthless. First, I am a complex human being, far too complex to merit the generalized rating of worthlessness. Second, even if I do say something mundane about my research, this is one aspect of my work as an academic and one aspect of my complex ongoing totality. It is unrealistic and illogical for me to conclude that I am worthless based on this evidence, and the same is the case if my colleagues doubt my academic credibility. While my academic reputation is important to me, it certainly does not and cannot define me as a person.

Finally, as long as I hold this irrational belief, I will perpetuate my anxiety problem because I will not take the risk to talk about my research and I will look for ways of leaving the party at the first sign of trouble. These safety-seeking behaviours will impede me in letting go of my anxiety in this situation and others like it.

3 State the alternative specific rational belief:

I really don't want others at the party to question my academic credibility if I say something mundane about my research, but this does not mean that they must not do so. If they do, it may be disadvantageous to me, but it would not prove that I am worthless. I am the same complex fallible human being whether or not they doubt my academic credibility.

4 Give reasons why this specific rational belief is rational:

It is true that I really don't want my colleagues at the party to doubt my academic credibility if I say something mundane about my research and it is also true that there is no law decreeing that they must not do so. If there were such a law it would be impossible for them to harbour negative thoughts about me as an academic. Since they have the freedom to think negatively of me, this proves that no such law exists.

It is also true that I am the same fallible person no matter what their opinion is about me as an academic. I can prove that it may well be disadvantageous to me if they harbour negative thoughts about me as an academic, because they express these opinions and this may affect my reputation. But my worth as a person, if it depends on anything, depends on my uniqueness, my fallibility and my aliveness, not – I repeat, not! – on my academic reputation.

If I hold and rehearse this rational belief when I go to the party, I will confront the possibility that my colleagues may doubt my academic credibility if I say something mundane about my research by speaking up about it and even introducing the topic if nobody else mentions it. Confronting my problem in this situation and others like it will help me to face, address and eventually let go of my anxiety.

Phil reviewed the above arguments before going to the party and did raise the topic of his research, which he discussed with his colleagues for about ten minutes. On reviewing what he said, he did think that he made a few mundane points and as he thought about this he practised his specific rational belief after the fact.

Step 9 Phil confronts threat sensibly, while rehearsing rational beliefs and while thinking realistically and acting healthily

Phil followed the general guidance about confronting threat that I discussed earlier in this chapter. Thus, with both problems, Phil acted on the 'challenging, but not overwhelming' principle. For example, after talking about his research to his colleagues in informal gatherings such as the party discussed above, Phil talked about it in more formal academic settings: first, with graduate students, then with academic colleagues in his own department and then with academic peers in other universities. Finally, he gave formal presentations on his research at national and international conferences. He made extensive use of the imagery method that I mentioned on page 30, where he pictured himself thinking rationally about the possibility of being judged negatively as an academic (see Chapter 3, pages 73 and 75, for a more extended example).

While rehearsing his rational beliefs in imagery and in real-life settings, Phil made use of the constructive behaviour and realistic thinking that he outlined when he re-did his situational ABC based on his rational beliefs, as shown below.

Situation

I am going to a drinks party attended by a number of my academic colleagues.

A = Activating event

Others questioning my academic credibility if I say something mundane about my research.

B = Rational belief

I really don't want others at the party to question my academic credibility if I say something mundane about my research, but this does not mean that they must not do so. If they do, it may be disadvantageous to me, but it would not prove that I am worthless. I am the same complex fallible human being whether or not they doubt my academic credibility.

C = Consequences of the irrational beliefs at B about the activating event at A

Emotional C = Concern

Behavioural C = Preparing what I am going to say if the topic of my research comes up, but not overpreparing.
Keeping to the subject if the topic of my research comes up.
Staying in the situation if I say something mundane.

Thinking C = Thinking that some of my colleagues may think I am a fraud if I don't sparkle, others will be understanding, yet others will take a neutral view and some may not even notice.
Realizing that while it could happen that my

> reputation will be more widely damaged if I say something mundane about my research, it is highly unlikely that such a negative result could follow from what is objectively a minor negative event.

For example, thinking-wise, Phil kept the likelihood of his reputation being damaged in realistic perspective and reminded himself that any mundane points he made when discussing his research would yield a mixed response from his colleagues. Behaviourally, he made sure that he did not change the subject if asked about his research and that he didn't act on any urges to avoid the possibility of making mundane points. Indeed, later on in counselling, after he had made quite a lot of progress in developing conviction in his rational beliefs, I encouraged him to deliberately make such mundane points to see what actually happened when he did so.

Step 10 Phil deals with the thinking consequences of irrational beliefs

Once Phil had developed a reasonable level of conviction in his rational beliefs, he noticed that his subsequent thinking became more realistic. Thus, as he accepted himself in the face of possible negative judgments by his students for showing that he was anxious in lectures, he recognized that, should he show such anxiety, he would get a range of reactions from his students, not just negative ones. However, he still had thoughts and images of people discussing what a weirdo he was in student coffee bars weeks later. He first assumed that this was true, practised accepting himself in the face of this and then practised mindfully accepting such thoughts as the slow-to-extinguish vestiges of his irrational belief. As such he let these thoughts and images come into and go out of his mind without actively engaging with them and without trying to get rid of them. He thus used a combination of Options 2 and 5 in dealing with the thinking consequences of his irrational beliefs which I discussed on pages 32 and 35–6.

Step 11 Phil commits himself to confront threat on a regular basis and generalize his learning

In the section on confronting threat sensibly, I discussed how Phil took sensible steps in confronting his anxiety of being regarded as a fraud by his academic colleagues. He took similar sensible 'challenging, but not overwhelming' steps in confronting his anxiety of being regarded as abnormal by his students. The work that he did in these two areas showed that he understood and acted on the principle of confronting threat regularly. As he did so, he practised rehearsing his rational beliefs while acting and thinking in ways that reflected these beliefs. These two principles of regular and consistent practice were perhaps the two most important ingredients of Phil letting go of his anxiety. Since Phil only had these two anxiety problems he did not need to generalize his learning to other problem areas.

Step 12 Phil deals with his obstacles to making progress

Phil had two major obstacles to making progress in letting go of his anxiety. The first occurred at the beginning of counselling. Perhaps unsurprisingly, Phil considered himself to be abnormal for having to seek help for his problems. However, when he saw that many people had similar problems and that this did not prove that there were many abnormal people out there, only ordinary people suffering from common problems of anxiety, Phil let go of the idea that he was abnormal for seeking help and engaged in the process of counselling.

The second obstacle to change that Phil encountered was perhaps in keeping with his academic approach to life, in that he held the view that once he understood the ideas behind the REBT approach to letting go of anxiety, he thought that he could automatically and easily implement these ideas in his own life. Once Phil appreciated that understanding these ideas was the launching pad for change and did not bring change itself, he resolved to undertake a graded approach to confronting his fears, as documented above. When he did so he was very diligent in implementing REBT in addressing the twin threats of being judged negatively by his students and by his colleagues.

Step 13 Phil's new non-anxious world view

Based on the work that Phil and I did on his problems in counselling, Phil let go of his anxiety about showing weakness in front of his students and his staff colleagues. He began to see that when he came across in a less than ideal way in academic settings, it was far from inevitable that he would be judged negatively. He learned that exposure of so-called weakness led to a variety of responses in others, some judgmental (which he increasingly handled in a rational manner), some neutral and some sympathetic. He also realized that others did not even register his 'weak' behaviour.

As a result, Phil developed the following non-anxious world view that was relevant to his problems and which I contrast with his previous anxious world view. In the later phase of counselling, Phil began to put his view of himself as an academic in a much healthier context, with the result that he not only became more relaxed within academic settings, but he also became more fulfilled outside it. His life became richer and less tense all round.

Phil's anxious world view	**Phil's non-anxious world view**
Public exposure of weakness is highly dangerous and must be avoided at all costs.	Public exposure can be dangerous, but not intrinsically so. When it is, I can still handle it by thinking rationally and realistically about it and by acting constructively with others who judge me negatively.
Academic life is a jungle where you have to be totally in control to survive.	Academic life has its joys and its stresses, but it is not a dog-eat-dog jungle. I can approach it as I am – a fallible human being who is bright, who can be mundane and who can be anxious – and enjoy some of it while disliking other aspects. My life is defined by being an academic.
My life is defined by being an academic.	Being an academic is an important aspect of my life, but is not the be-all and end-all of my life.

In the next chapter, I will show you how you can let go of depression.

3

How to Let Go of Depression

Depression is the other of the two most frequently experienced psychological problems, the first one being anxiety, which I discussed in the previous chapter. Once again you can let go of depression by understanding the dynamics of this debilitating emotion (i.e. how it works) and rigorously (but not rigidly) following a number of important psychological principles based on the psychology of sadness or disappointment which are the healthy alternatives to depression.

UNDERSTANDING THE DYNAMICS OF DEPRESSION AND SADNESS/ DISAPPOINTMENT

The following points show how depression and sadness/disappointment work.

- When you experience psychologically based depression (rather than depression that stems from non-psychological sources) explicitly or implicitly you think that you have *lost* something important from your personal domain or have *failed* within this domain. Your personal domain contains people, objects, principles and hopes – to name but a few – that are important to you. This helps you to see the difference between anxiety and depression. Anxiety is about threat that has yet to happen, whereas depression is about loss or failure that has happened. You may well experience both.
- Applying the REBT model which I outlined in Chapter 1, perception of loss or failure *does not* cause depression. Rather, depression stems from a set of irrational beliefs about loss and failure. Sadness and disappointment stem from a set of rational beliefs about loss and failure. I will amplify these important points later in this chapter.
- As I first discussed in Chapter 2, irrational beliefs can be specific or general. When they are specific, these irrational beliefs are held in specific situations. When they are general, they are held across

relevant situations. Rational beliefs can also be general or specific and similar points apply.

- When you hold a general irrational belief, you bring this to specific situations that could possibly embody the loss or failure theme of the irrational belief. When you do so, you tend to infer the presence of loss or failure in the absence of good corroborative evidence. For example, let's assume that you hold the following general irrational belief: 'I must be outstandingly successful at any significant task I tackle,' and bring this to your performance on a specific significant task. In doing so, you are more likely to infer that you will fail at the task than you would if your general belief was rational. Holding the latter will lead you to infer the prospect of failure only if there were clear objective evidence indicating that you would probably fail.

  As I have just shown, bringing a general rational belief to specific situations that could embody the loss or failure theme would lead to inferences about the presence of loss or failure when it was objectively clear that loss or failure was present.

  It follows from this that one way of staying relatively free from depression is to hold general rational beliefs about loss and failure rather than general irrational beliefs about loss and failure.
- As I discussed in Chapter 1, in REBT we often (but not always) encourage our clients to assume temporarily that their inferences are true (see page 26). We do this to help our clients and ourselves identify the underlying irrational beliefs that are at the core of their psychological difficulties and see that they have a choice concerning whether to think irrationally or rationally about these inferences – in the case of depression and sadness/disappointment, inferences of loss and failure.
- In order to make an informed choice on this issue, you need to understand the consequences of holding irrational and rational beliefs about loss and failure. Table 2 lists these consequences.
- If you look at Table 2, you will see that most of the behavioural consequences of loss-related and failure-related irrational beliefs are designed to remove you from the source of your depression, but in a way that actually perpetuates your depressed feelings. This is because the majority of such actions are inactive in nature, and since depression 'thrives' on inactivity this will perpetuate your black mood. Second, although you are inactive, your mind isn't, and as you can see from Table 2, the thinking consequences of your depression-creating irrational beliefs are highly negative, leading to your depression being intensified.

Irrational beliefs about loss/ failure	**Rational beliefs about loss/ failure**
Emotional consequences	***Emotional consequences***
– Depression	– Sadness, disappointment
Behavioural consequences	***Behavioural consequences***
– Withdraw from reinforcements	– Seek out reinforcements after a period of mourning
– Withdraw into oneself	– Maintain connection with others
– Do not talk about feelings	– Express feelings about loss/ failure and discuss these with significant others
– Attempt to cling on to others	– Accept support from others, but not in a clinging way
– Create a negative environment consistent with depressed feelings	– Maintain an environment that takes into account loss/failure, but which includes positive features
– Attempt to terminate feelings of depression in self-destructive ways	– Stay with feelings of sadness or disappointment and deal with them constructively
Thinking consequences	***Thinking consequences***
– See only negative aspects of the loss/failure	– Able to see both positive and negative of the loss/failure
– Think of other losses/failures experienced	– Can think of gains/successes experienced as well as losses/ failures
– Think one is unable to help oneself (helplessness)	– Able to help self (resourcefulness)
– Can only see pain, blackness and emptiness in the future (hopelessness)	– Able to look to the future with realistic optimism (hope)

Table 2 Consequences of irrational and rational beliefs about loss/failure

- Most of the thinking consequences of loss-related and failure-related irrational beliefs lead you to think that your life in particular, and the world in general, is far more negative that it actually is and that you are far more helpless to improve things than you actually are. On the other hand, the thinking consequences of loss-related and failure-related rational beliefs lead you to be more realistic in your appraisal of the complexity of your life and that of the world on the one hand, and in your ability to help improve your lot on the other.

- As the above two points show, when you think irrationally about loss or failure you swing between trying to withdraw from the source of your pain and thinking that your life in particular, and the world in general, is bleak. Neither of these positions actually helps you to deal effectively with loss or failure in the long term. On the other hand, when you think rationally about loss and failure you are able to face up to and digest the loss or failure you have experienced, put it into a healthy perspective and re-engage with life.
- Assuming that you have chosen to think rationally, rather than irrationally, about loss and failure, you are now ready to work towards letting go of depression.

14 STEPS TO LETTING GO OF DEPRESSION

In this section, I outline a number of steps that you need to take in order to let go of depression. Once again, before I outline and describe these steps, I want to make two important points. First, I do not mean to imply that all the steps are essential and that if you miss any out, you will not make any progress in overcoming your depression. My view is that none of the steps is essential, but the more steps you follow the more likely it is that you will become relatively free from depression. Second, the order in which the steps are presented is not set in stone, but is just the most logical as I see it. You may find that a different order works better for you. If so, fine. Experiment and see for yourself.

Step 1 Admit that you experience depression and that it is a problem for you

It is important that you admit that you suffer from depression and that it is a problem for you. These are in fact separate steps. You may, for example, admit that you experience depression, but you may not see it as a problem for you. Thus, you may think that your feelings of depression are a sign of great sensitivity, and that not to have them means you are indifferent to negative life events. If so, you need to see that healthy sadness is a sign of sensitivity, but sensitivity without disturbance. Depression is a sign of disturbed oversensitivity and if you felt sad, but not depressed, about a loss, for example, you would still be sensitive, but healthily so.

Step 2 See that sadness (or disappointment) is a viable alternative to depression

If you are going to work towards letting go of depression, then it is important that you see clearly that there is a realistic and plausible alternative to this emotion. This alternative is known as sadness (with respect to loss) or disappointment (with respect to failure). As you will see from Table 2, sadness and disappointment stem from rational beliefs about loss and failure respectively (whereas depression stems from irrational beliefs about loss/failure), and these two emotions accompany a set of behavioural and thinking consequences of loss-related and failure-related rational beliefs that are far more constructive than the behavioural and thinking consequences of irrational beliefs about loss and failure that accompany depression.

Step 3 Accept yourself for feeling depression

Once you have admitted that you suffer from depression and that it is a problem for you, it is important that you accept yourself for having depressed feelings and refrain from depreciating yourself for experiencing depression. Show yourself that you are not a weak person or a disturbed person for feeling depressed. If you must see depression as a weakness, that is your prerogative; it can be seen as a disturbance in that it will interfere with the quality of your life, but this weakness or disturbance does not prove that you are a weak person or a disturbed person, unless you choose to define yourself as such. Rather, it proves that you are an ordinary fallible human being who, along with millions of others, suffers from depression. Accepting yourself in this way will help you to focus on the task at hand, which is to work towards letting go of depression. Depreciating yourself for feeling depressed again gives you two problems for the price of one and certainly doesn't help you to deal constructively with your depression.

Step 4 Identify themes to your depression

The next step is for you to identify what you routinely feel depressed about. As you do this, you might find it helpful to distinguish between what professionals call autonomous depression and sociotropic depression. Basically, you experience autonomous depression when you prize personal effectiveness and freedom and you hold irrational beliefs about a loss or failure within part of your personal domain. On the other hand, you experience sociotropic depression when you prize your relationships with valued others and you hold irrational beliefs about some loss within this aspect of your personal domain. The following makes clear the difference.

Themes in autonomous depression:
- failure;
- goals blocked;
- loss of status;
- loss of autonomy;
- inability to do prized activities (e.g. because of sudden disability);
- being dependent on others;
- loss of choice;
- loss of self-control.

Themes in sociotropic depression:
- disapproval;
- rejection;
- criticism;
- loss of love;
- negative evaluation from others;
- losing connection with significant others;
- being on one's own;
- loss of reputation or social standing.

Use these lists to identify what you feel depressed about.

Step 5 Identify your general depression-related irrational beliefs

With the above information you should now be ready to identify the general irrational beliefs that underpin your depression. What you do is to bring together the above identified themes with the relevant irrational beliefs that I discussed in detail in Chapter 1. If you recall, these are as follows:

- rigid demands (e.g. musts, absolute shoulds, oughts, got to's, etc.);
- awfulizing beliefs (e.g. It's awful that . . . , It's terrible that . . . , It's the end of the world that . . . , etc.);
- low frustration tolerance (LFT) beliefs (e.g. I can't bear it, I can't stand it, It's intolerable, etc.);
- depreciation beliefs. There are two types of depreciation beliefs relevant to depression: self-depreciation beliefs (e.g. I am worthless, I am a bad person, I am inadequate, etc.) and life-depreciation beliefs (e.g. Life is bad).

When formulating general irrational beliefs that underpin your depression, I suggest the following two principles:

Principle 1

If your depression is primarily ego-based, meaning that when you are depressed a prime component to your depression is that you depreciate yourself as a person, then include the following components in formulating your general irrational belief:

- theme related to loss or failure;
- demanding belief + self-depreciation belief.

Here are a few examples, together with their emotional, behavioural and thinking consequences:

General loss-related or failure-related irrational belief: ego-based	Consequences of GiB
I must not fail at important tasks, and as I have I am a failure.	– Depression on having failed the task – Predicting a bleak future full of failure – Overestimating the negative consequences of failure

	– Avoiding attempting similar tasks – Thinking about other past failures
I must be loved and since I think I am not, I am unlovable.	– Depression about being unloved – Predicting a bleak loveless future – Thinking about my unlovable aspects and that I have no redeeming features – Withdrawing from others

Principle 2

If your depression is primarily non-ego-based, meaning that when you are depressd a prime component to your depression does not involve you depreciating yourself as a person, then include the following components in formulating your general irrational belief:

- theme related to loss or failure;
- demanding belief + awfulizing belief or LFT belief.

Here are a few examples, together with their emotional, behavioural and thinking consequences:

General loss-related or failure-related irrational belief: non-ego-based	**Consequences of GiB**
I must not be dependent on others and as I am it is terrible.	– Depression about being dependent – Thinking of things I can't do on my own and not about what I can do

	– Thinking that my future is bleak without my independence – Alternating between giving up on helping myself and refusing to accept help from others even when it is in my healthy interests to do so – Thinking that others feel pity for me and thus stay away from them
I must not lose the comfort of being looked after and I can't bear it now I have lost this.	– Feeling depressed when I think that I have nobody to look after me – Underestimating what I can do on my own – Acting helpless to get others to help me – Thinking that nobody will look after me again – Withdrawing from enjoyable activities

Step 6 Challenge your general loss-related and failure-related irrational beliefs, then develop and rehearse an alternative set of general rational beliefs

In order to let go of depression, it is important that you operate according to a set of general rational beliefs about loss or failure. In order to do this you need to weaken your conviction in your general irrational beliefs about loss or failure and develop and strengthen your conviction in an alternative set of general rational beliefs.

I suggest that you re-read Chapter 1 and particularly the material on pages 2–10 where I go over arguments why demands, awfulizing beliefs, LFT beliefs and depreciation beliefs are irrational, and why full preferences, non-awfulizing beliefs, HFT beliefs and acceptance beliefs are rational. Then you can apply similar arguments to your general irrational and rational beliefs about loss and failure. In doing so I suggest that you use the following format:

1 State your general irrational belief.
2 Give reasons why your general irrational belief is irrational.
3 State the alternative general rational belief.
4 Give reasons why your general rational belief is rational.

Here is an example of how to do this.

The case of Fred

Here is how Fred used the four guidelines to help him develop a healthy general rational belief about being made redundant, which he thought meant that he was no longer productive.

1 State your general irrational belief:

I must be productive and I am useless because I am not.

2 Give reasons why your general irrational belief is irrational:

Sadly, there is no law of the universe that decrees that I must always be productive. I am not exempt from periods of being unproductive even though I would like to be. If I were exempt, it would have been impossible for me to lose my job. Since I have lost my job this rigid law does not exist.

Even if it can be said that I am not being productive having lost my job, this does not prove that I am useless as a person. My lack of so-called productivity is a transitory state and cannot define my identity, which is far too complex to be defined by this state. For me to be useless as a person, I would have to be useless at everything that I did, which is far, far from the truth. Also, even if losing my job means that I am unproductive at the moment, this does not prove that I am useless, since this would mean that a part of me (i.e. my temporary non-productivity) can define the whole of me. This is the error of logic known as the part–whole error.

Also, as long as I hold this general irrational belief, then I will be depressed whenever I am not doing anything that I consider to be productive and I will act and think in depressed ways consistent with this belief.

3 State the alternative general rational belief:

I would much prefer it if I were productive, but it isn't essential that I am this way all the time. If I am unproductive this does not mean that I am useless. It means that I am an ordinary fallible human being capable of being productive and unproductive at different times.

4 Give reasons why your general rational belief is rational:

It is true both that I would prefer it if I were productive and that I am not exempt from non-productivity. Also, it is true that my non-productivity proves that I am a fallible human being capable of being productive and unproductive. My worth as a person can never truly be defined by how productive I am at a given point in time.

If I develop and hold my general rational belief, then I will be disappointed, but not depressed, about losing my job and being unproductive, and I will act and think in non-depressed ways consistent with this belief.

Follow the above four guidelines, review your arguments regularly and rehearse your general rational belief. As you develop greater conviction in your general rational belief about loss and failure, you will find that you will increasingly bring it to situations where you might experience a loss or a failure and you will make much more realistic appraisals of what will happen and your ability to deal productively with it. As such, you will take more risks and live a more active life, which is itself a good antidote to depression.

Step 7 Analyse specific episodes of depression

When you begin to feel psychologically depressed, this is usually in response to a particular trigger representing loss or failure that occurs in a specific situation and when you hold specific irrational beliefs about loss or failure. As this is the case, you need a format in which to assess the important factors that are involved in your specific depressed response as a prelude to you learning to overcome your situationally based depression. As in Chapter 2, I suggest the following situational ABC framework.

Situation

We do not react in a vacuum. Rather, we think, feel and act in specific situations. The term 'situation' in the 'situational ABC model' refers to a descriptive account of the actual event to which we respond emotionally and behaviourally.

Describe the situation in which you were depressed as objectively as possible.

A = Activating event

Within this specific situation, when you are depressed it is usually about some key or critical aspect of this situation which you perceive as a loss or a failure. This is known as the activating event.

Ask yourself the following: What aspect of the situation I have just described was I most depressed about or did I see as a loss or a failure? (Assume temporarily that your A is true. The best time to question the validity of A is when you are thinking rationally about it.)

B = Irrational belief

Remember that in REBT A does not cause your depression. Rather, your depression is primarily determined by the beliefs that you hold about A.

For a loss or failure that primarily 'lowered your self-esteem', write down your demanding belief and your associated self-depreciation belief. For a loss or failure that did not primarily 'lower your self-esteem', write down your demanding belief and either your awfulizing belief or your low frustration tolerance belief.

C = Consequences of the irrational beliefs at B about the activating event at A

When you hold a belief about an activating event at A, you will tend to experience an emotion, you will tend to act in a certain way and you will tend to think in certain ways. These three consequences of this AxB interaction are known as emotional, behavioural and thinking consequences respectively.

Identify your depression (emotional consequence), the way you acted or felt like acting while feeling depressed (behavioural consequences) and how you thought while feeling depressed (thinking consequences).

Let's now see how one person used the ABC model to analyse a specific episode of depression.

The case of Joyce

Situation = My boyfriend told me that he wanted to go out with his mates rather than come to my friend's wedding with me.

Activating event (aspect of the situation that I was most anxious about) = My boyfriend does not care for me.

B (Irrational beliefs) = My boyfriend must care for me and I am unlovable because he doesn't.

C (Consequences of BxA)

Emotional (unhealthy negative) = Depression

Behavioural (unconstructive) = 1 Go to bed and don't go to wedding.
2 Don't talk about my feelings to friends.
3 Avoid my boyfriend.

Thinking (unrealistic and skewed) = 1 Thinking that boyfriend will reject me soon.
2 Thinking that I will end up an old maid.

Step 8 Challenge your specific loss-related or failure-related irrational beliefs, then develop and rehearse an alternative set of specific rational beliefs

Having accurately assessed the factors associated with your situationally based depression, you are now ready to challenge your specific loss-related or failure-related irrational beliefs and to develop their specific rational alternatives. To do this you use similar guidelines to the ones that I outlined in Step 6 above. Applying these guidelines to challenging specific beliefs, we have:

1 State your specific irrational belief.
2 Give reasons why your specific irrational belief is irrational.
3 State the alternative specific rational belief.
4 Give reasons why your specific rational belief is rational.

Here is how Joyce used the four guidelines to help develop alternative specific rational beliefs about her boyfriend wanting to go out with his mates rather than to her friend's wedding:

1 State your specific irrational belief:

My boyfriend must care for me and I am unlovable because he doesn't.

2 Give reasons why your specific irrational belief is irrational:

If there were a law of the universe that stated that my boyfriend must care for me then he would care for me and want to come with me to my friend's wedding, no matter what. Unfortunately, there is no law, and as long as I demand that there is one, I will be depressed. Also, it is not true that I am unlovable if my boyfriend does not care for me. I am not unlovable because I am able to be loved and this cannot be wiped out by my boyfriend's lack of caring for me. If I believe that it can then I will be depressed.

3 State the alternative specific rational belief:

I want my boyfriend to care for me, but he doesn't have to do so. His lack of caring does not mean that I am unlovable. It means that he does not care for me and this cannot change my lovability. I am lovable no matter what, even though I may have some qualities that my boyfriend doesn't appreciate.

4 Give reasons why your specific rational belief is rational:

It is true that I want my boyfriend to care for me and it is also true that he doesn't have to do so, since he has the power of choice to care for me or not. Believing this will lead me to feel sadness rather than depression about his lack of caring. I can also prove that I am lovable, meaning able to be loved, despite my boyfriend's lack of caring. If I was unlovable no one could possibly love me, which is hardly the case.

Believing this will also lead me to feel sad, but not depressed, by my boyfriend's uncaring response.

Once you have followed these guidelines, rehearse your specific rational belief and then move on to the next step.

Step 9 Mourn your loss or failure and then get on with life, while rehearsing rational beliefs and while thinking realistically and acting healthily

This step is perhaps the most important one of all. After you have gained some experience of challenging your specific loss-related or failure-related irrational belief, it is important for you to mourn your loss and then get on with life. By mourning, I mean a process where you allow yourself to fully experience your feelings of sadness and disappointment, where you then put the loss or failure that you experienced into an overall perspective on your life, and then you get on with your life. As you do so, it is important that you rehearse your specific rational belief and that you act and think in ways that are consistent with this specific belief. The best way of determining constructive ways of acting and thinking is to re-do your situational ABC, this time based on holding a specific rational belief.

The case of Joyce revisited

Here is how Joyce re-did her ABC.

Situation = My boyfriend told me that he wanted to go out with his mates rather than come to my friend's wedding with me.

A = My boyfriend does not care for me.

B (Rational beliefs) = I want my boyfriend to care for me, but he doesn't have to do so. His lack of caring does not mean that I am unlovable. It means that he does not care for me and this cannot change my lovability. I am lovable no matter what, even though I may have some qualities that my boyfriend doesn't appreciate.

C = Emotional (healthy negative) = Sadness

Behavioural (constructive) =
1 Talk to my best friend about my feelings of sadness.
2 Keep out of bed and go to wedding.
3 Talk to my boyfriend about his reasons for not wanting to go to the wedding.

Thinking (realistic and balanced) =
1 Thinking that my boyfriend's not wanting to go to my friend's wedding may mean other things than him not caring for me.
2 If he does not care for me and wants to end the relationship, thinking that I will be able to have other relationships.

How Joyce mourned her loss and got on with life

Once Joyce had re-done her situational ABC, she decided that while it would be sad if her boyfriend didn't care enough for her, it wouldn't be terrible. However, since she would miss him she sat down and allowed herself to experience her sad feelings and then discussed the incident with her best friend, who put it to her that just because her boyfriend preferred to go out with his mates rather than to her friend's wedding, this didn't mean that he didn't care for her. Her friend put forward the view that it could mean anything, such as that he disliked formal gatherings. Because Joyce had challenged and changed her irrational belief about her boyfriend's presumed lack of care, she was receptive to this different perspective on his behaviour and resolved to discuss it with him after going to the wedding.

This is a very good illustration of why in REBT we encourage you to assume temporarily that the inferences that you make at A in the ABC when you are depressed are true. We do this so that you can identify, challenge and change your irrational belief about the actual or presumed loss or failure at A which is at the core of your depression. If Joyce had discussed the situation with her friend while still in the grip of her irrational belief about her boyfriend's presumed 'uncaring' attitude towards her, she would not have been open to her friend's suggested alternative explanation of her boyfriend's behaviour, since her still active irrational belief would have led her to continue to think in unrealistic and negatively skewed ways. Having challenged her irrational belief about her boyfriend's behaviour, she was operating on her rational belief, and thus was in a more realistic and balanced frame of mind and was open to questioning her original interpretation at A.

General comments about mourning loss and failure and getting on with life

I want to make the following points about mourning the losses and failures that you experience in life and then getting on with your life. In making these points, I assume that you have challenged your irrational beliefs about loss or failure, and are holding the relevant irrational beliefs and feeling sad about your loss or disappointed about your failure.

- It takes time to mourn, and it is important that you realize that different people mourn at different rates and at different levels of intensity. Allow yourself to mourn in a way that is natural to you and not according to the timetable of others.

- When you mourn your losses and failures, you may find it important to remain connected to people you care for and who care for you. You may want to talk about how you feel to such people, or you may just want their company and simply 'hang out' with them. The important thing is that you keep connected in whatever way you find therapeutic.
- You may, however, gain solace from being on your own. Thus, you may find it useful to take long walks by yourself or engage in solitary activities that help you to get your loss or failure into perspective. The important factor is that you know how you can best mourn your loss or failure and get on with your life.
- As you mourn your loss or failure, you may well find it a struggle to hold on to your rational belief and related constructive behaviour and realistic thinking. If you stick with the struggle, you will succeed in the end, but it will be a struggle. Don't expect to masterfully and easily hold on to your rational belief, etc. If you hold such an expectation, you will not do the necessary work that you need to do to gain conviction in your rational belief.
- As part of this struggle, you may well experience the urge to act in your usual unhealthy way and your initial thoughts may be unrealistic. If you accept that this will happen and that you need to persist in keeping your rational belief in the forefront of your mind, while acting in constructive but unaccustomed ways and while keeping your thoughts balanced and realistic, then you will increase your conviction in your rational beliefs.

Step 10 Confront potential losses and failures in your mind's eye and then in reality

As I have already discussed, one of the features of depression is inactivity and lack of risk-taking. The latter is perhaps understandable. If you think that you will fail if you try something – and, more than this, that you will depress yourself with your failure – then it perhaps makes sense to avoid taking risks. This is a double-edged sword and you cut yourself on each edge. First, by not taking risks you deprive yourself of the possibility of getting your goals met, whether they are autonomous goals (e.g. advancement at work or going self-employed) or sociotropic goals (e.g. asking out for a date someone you have admired from afar, or deepening a superficial friendship). By not pursuing your goals, you reinforce your depressed view that life is bleak. By not taking sensible risks you implicitly reinforce your irrational beliefs about loss or failure. In effect, in not taking risks you are saying the following, for example: 'While I would dearly like to ask this person out for a date I am not going to do so, because if I asked her and she said no this would be terrible. I must not be rejected and if she rejects me this proves that I am worthless.' This is what Ralph did until I taught him how to use REBT to help himself.

The first step to reverse this process and become more adventurous in life, so that you at least have a chance of achieving your goals, is to practise your developing rational beliefs while imagining that you have experienced a significant loss or failure. Here is how Ralph did this. First, he got his rational belief about being rejected clear in his mind. In fact, he wrote this belief down on a card and had it in front of him. It read: 'I really would prefer not to be rejected by this woman, but that doesn't mean that she must not reject me. If she does reject me, then this would be bad, but it would certainly not prove that I am worthless. I am still the same fallible human being whether she decides to go out with me or not. It's better if she goes out with me, but my worth stays the same whatever happens.'

Then, Ralph closed his eyes and vividly imagined asking the woman out on a date and being turned down. As he imagined this happening, he rehearsed the above rational belief, reading it if necessary, until he felt sad and disappointed, but not depressed, about being rejected. He then stayed with these feelings of sadness and disappointment for about five minutes, all the time rehearsing his rational belief while imagining being turned down. He repeated this about four times a day for a month and then felt ready to ask the woman out for a date.

After you have done something similar, it is important that you then actually take a risk in real life while again rehearsing the rational belief that you practised in the above described imagery technique. As you do so it is important that you act and think in ways that are consistent with your rational belief and refrain from acting and thinking in ways that were associated with your previously held irrational belief. Consult Table 2 on page 59 if you need any help in identifying the behavioural and thinking consequences of both your rational belief and your irrational belief.

This is what Ralph did. He decided to actually approach Samantha and ask her for a date. He rehearsed his rational belief about her saying no before asking her, and kept this belief in mind as he did so. Previously, if he had plucked up the courage to ask her out, he would have done so in a roundabout way to minimize the 'pain' of rejection (safety behavioural consequence of irrational belief). This time, he asked her out directly and unequivocally (behavioural consequence of rational belief). Previously he would have thought that if Samantha said no to a date, then this would mean that nobody would go out with him (thinking consequence of irrational belief). This time, along with his rehearsal of his rational belief he thought that if Samantha turned him down, then others would still be prepared to go out with him (thinking consequence of rational belief). Note how Ralph rehearsed his rational belief and acted and thought in ways that were consistent with his rational belief. This is the best way of strengthening your conviction in your developing rational belief.

Step 11 How to deal with the thinking consequences of irrational beliefs

There is one important point about depression that you need to bear in mind. You begin by depressing yourself about a loss or a failure at A and then you create other losses or failures at C as a consequence of holding irrational beliefs. These losses or failures are usually much more exaggerated than those at A that trigger irrational beliefs. Here are a few examples that will clarify what I mean:

Example 1

A (loss): My friend thinks less of me.

B (irrational belief): My friend must not think less of me and as she does it proves that I am unlikeable.

C (thinking consequence: new loss): All of my friends will dislike me.

Example 2

A (failure): I failed to get promoted at work.

B (irrational belief): I absolutely should have been promoted and it is terrible that I wasn't.

C (thinking consequence: new failure): I will never better myself vocationally.

As these examples show, you start out with a loss or failure at A and end up with a more negative loss or failure in your mind at C, because you hold an irrational belief at B about the original loss or failure at A. Once you have made this connection between the original loss/failure at A and the exaggerated thinking consequence at C via your irrational belief, and you have rehearsed this connection a number of times, you very quickly think of the exaggerated scenario whenever you think of the original loss or failure. Applying this to the above examples:

1 Whenever the person thinks that her friend dislikes her, she very quickly thinks that all her friends dislike her.
2 Whenever the person fails to gain some advancement at work, he thinks that he will never do so.

So far, I have urged you to assume temporarily that the loss or failure that you have experienced at A is real so that you can identify, challenge and change your irrational belief at B. But how can you best deal with the thinking consequences of your irrational beliefs? Let me begin by outlining your options and consider the issues that emerge from each of these options. These options are similar to the ones that I discussed regarding anxiety in Chapter 2.

Option 1 Go back to challenge your irrational belief

When you think that you will face a very exaggerated loss or failure, understand that this is evidence that you are operating on an irrational belief about a prior less exaggerated loss or failure. Use this as a cue to go back to challenge this irrational belief.

Option 2 Let the thoughts be and allow them to pass through your mind

When you think that you will face a very exaggerated loss or failure and you have challenged the irrational belief about the prior less exaggerated loss or failure (see above), understand that these exaggerated thoughts are vestiges of this irrational belief and that they will eventually go if you do not engage with them or act on them. Rather, treat them as cars passing you by as you stand on a street corner. In other words, allow these thoughts to come into your mind and go out the other side without engaging with them in thought or in deed.

Option 3 Question the realism of the thinking consequence

When you think that you are facing a very exaggerated loss or failure, question how realistic it is, given the actual situation you are in. Thus, if you think that your friend dislikes you, ask yourself how likely it is that all your friends will dislike you. If a close friend told you that she thought one friend disliked her and told you that this meant that all of her friends would soon dislike her, would you agree with her? What would be a more realistic conclusion instead? Such a conclusion is usually more balanced. In this case, a more realistic balanced conclusion would be something like: 'Just because I think that one friend dislikes me, it certainly does not follow that all my friends will dislike me, unless I have some very unfortunate habit that would alienate very many people, in which case I would have already lost all of my friends.'

Scholars have identified a number of thinking errors that characterize the thinking consequences of irrational beliefs. It is useful to identify the error and then come up with a more balanced alternative. I list the most common thinking errors in depression and their healthy antidotes below:

Error: Black and white thinking (e.g. 'Either I do well or I do poorly.')
Antidote: Continuum thinking (e.g. 'If I don't do well, I might do reasonably well or my performance might be average.')

Error: Hopelessness (e.g. 'If I do not do well now, then I will never do well.')
Antidote: Realistic hope (e.g. 'If I don't do well now, I may do well later if I learn from any mistakes that I may make.')

Error: Helplessness (e.g. 'If things go badly at work, I won't be able to put it right.')
Antidote: Realistic resourcefulness ('If things go badly at work, I may be able to put it right. If I am not able to, I can learn new skills that will help me.')

Once you have identified the error in your thinking consequence, develop an alternative thought based on the healthy antidote. Write both thoughts down on a piece of paper and ask yourself one or more of the following questions:

1 Which of these two thoughts is the more realistic?
2 If a friend had a similar experience, which of these two ways of thinking would I encourage my friend to adopt?
3 Which thought would a group of objective observers urge me to adopt?

4 Which thought will best help me over my depression?
5 Which is the more compassionate way of viewing the situation?

In Step 7, I showed you how to analyse a specific example of your depression. In doing so I encouraged you to assume temporarily that your A (the aspect of the situation about which you were most anxious) was true. I did this because this is the best way to identify your irrational belief that we in REBT argue is at the very core of your depression. In Step 7, I argued that the best time to question the validity of your A is when you are thinking rationally about it. Thus, after you have challenged your irrational belief about the A (Option 1) use the questions that I have outlined in this section to question the validity of your A (Option 3).

Please note one important point before I move on to Option 4. It is generally easier to implement Option 3 once you have carried out Option 1 (as suggested above).

Option 4 Conduct behavioural experiments

When you think that you will face a very exaggerated loss or failure it is important to test out in reality whether the loss or failure is real or not. As I discussed in the previous chapter, I fully appreciate that it 'feels' real, in the sense that when you have made yourself depressed the major thinking consequence of your irrational belief is an exaggerated loss or failure that you generally think will occur. However, as in anxiety, in depression it is important that you recognize that what 'feels' real or seems real may well be the unrealistic exaggerated thinking consequences of an irrational belief. As I have pointed out in Option 1, one way of distancing yourself from the very 'real' exaggerated loss or failure is to stand back and understand that this is a product of your irrational belief rather than an accurate reflection of the future. If you have challenged your irrational belief first, you will find this easier to do.

Sometimes this is not enough and you need to test out in reality whether the exaggerated loss or failure is real or not. Generally, this involves carrying out behavioural experiments where you confront the situation in reality without the use of any safety-seeking behaviours or thoughts. For example, if you think that all your friends will dislike you, then one way of testing this is to seek them out and see what happens without being extra nice to them, for example, in order to deliberately elicit a positive reaction from them. Experience can be a very powerful teacher, and if you do this a reasonable number of times you will learn the powerful lesson that your exaggerated thinking is a product of your irrational thinking, and is not a reliable guide to reality because it 'feels' or seems real.

With some exaggerated thinking at C, it is difficult to devise a behavioural experiment to disprove your negative prediction. Thus, if you think at C that you will become a 'bag lady' because you have upset one of your friends at A and you hold an irrational belief about this actual or presumed event, it is hard to devise an experiment to test this out and to disprove it. In such cases, it is important that you assess the probability of this happening while you are holding a rational belief about the original loss or failure at A. Instead, come up with a more probable event and assume that this is much more likely to happen. In doing so, you may have to challenge your need for a guarantee that the more exaggerated, but less likely, situation will not happen. Once you have done this you are more likely to accept the most probable outcome.

Option 5 Assume the thinking consequence will occur and think rationally about it

The final way of dealing with an exaggerated thinking consequence of an irrational belief is to assume temporarily that it will happen and to dispute your irrational belief about that consequence.

Since this may seem rather confusing, let me put it in diagrammatic form and provide an example. This example is the one I first introduced on page 75.

A (failure): I failed to get promoted at work.
B (irrational belief): I absolutely should have been promoted and it is terrible that I wasn't.
C (thinking consequence: new failure): I will never better myself vocationally.

↓

A (new failure): I will never better myself vocationally.
B (irrational belief): That would be dreadful. I couldn't tolerate that.

As this diagram shows, the person's exaggerated thinking consequence of his original irrational belief then becomes the new activating event on which he focuses and on which he bases another irrational belief. Using Option 5, the person would endeavour to show himself that if he never betters himself vocationally, then that would be a very bad situation indeed, but it still wouldn't be terrible. As I pointed out in Chapter 1 and again in Chapter 2, 'terrible' means, among other things, that nothing good could come out of the situation. This would not be true, since the person could, for example, devote his energies to non-work activities, particularly those that were meaningful to him, and attain the well-being he would experience if he was more successful at work. He could see thereby that his happiness is not dependent upon being a success vocationally, even though he might well be happier if he did succeed at work.

If the person was successful at disputing his irrational belief about not bettering himself vocationally, he would lose his depression about this highly aversive event, and in doing so he would be able to see that it is a grossly exaggerated event and one that is very unlikely to occur just because he failed on this occasion to be promoted.

Thinking rationally about highly aversive events that are in reality unlikely to occur (although always possible) is a great antidote to depression as well as anxiety. However, as you are probably thinking, it is difficult to do. Yet it is possible, and if you are prepared to work hard at thinking rationally you may well be able to think rationally even about the highly aversive events.

I did this in the early 1980s when I took redundancy from my job as Lecturer in Counselling at the University of Aston and received over 50 job rejections. I did not make myself depressed about this, partly because I showed myself that even if I never got a job again in counselling, this would certainly not be terrible because I could change tack vocationally and also get most of my satisfaction from non-work experiences. This philosophy helped me to keep applying for jobs, and it was not too long before I got a job offer from Goldsmiths College, where I still work eighteen years later.

Now, I am fully aware that not everyone reading this book will be able to think rationally about highly aversive life events. However, if you don't attempt this at all, you certainly won't succeed. So assume temporarily that a highly aversive event that you created through your irrational belief about the original loss or failure has occurred and work to think rationally about this. If you succeed you will make yourself far less vulnerable to depression, and you will keep striving to reach your goals rather than give up and see that such highly aversive events are unlikely to occur.

In this section, I have outlined five ways of dealing with the thinking consequences of your irrational beliefs. Become familiar with each of these options and use whichever method or methods (since you can use more than one) is/are most appropriate.

Step 12 Commit yourself to confront potential loss and failure on a regular basis and generalize your learning

So far I have outlined a number of important ingredients to letting go of depression. I have argued that it is important that you identify and challenge both your general and your specific loss-related and failure-related irrational beliefs and that you develop increasing conviction in your alternative rational beliefs. You can best do this by confronting loss or failure in imagination and, particularly, in reality while rehearsing your rational beliefs and while acting and thinking in ways that are consistent with these rational beliefs.

While doing this you need to understand that you may experience the urge to go back to well-established behavioural reactions to loss or failure that are largely designed to help you escape from what you consider to be the horrors of reality. Acting on these urges will lead you to escape in the short term, but will perpetuate your depression in the longer term because doing so does not give you opportunities to think rationally about loss and failure in the presence of these conditions. Thus, it is important for you to refrain from acting on these urges to seek immediate escape from what you see as reality, which is in all probability the distorted thinking consequences of your irrational beliefs.

I also argued that you need to understand how holding irrational beliefs about loss and failure can lead you very quickly to think of far more negative losses and failures and to think in general negative terms about yourself, your experiences and your future. I then outlined five approaches to responding constructively to these exaggerated thinking consequences of irrational beliefs.

If you follow these guidelines and apply them in a *repeated* and *consistent* manner to each of the themes that you identified earlier in the chapter about which you depress yourself, then you will assuredly make progress in letting go of depression.

I have stressed the terms 'repeated' and 'consistent' here for good reason. First, just facing a potential loss or failure once will not help you much, even though you are rehearsing a rational belief and acting and thinking in ways that are consistent with that belief. You need to do this a good number of times before your feelings change. As I discussed in Chapter 2, emotional change at first lags well behind behavioural and thinking change, but if you keep rehearsing your rational beliefs while confronting potential loss and failure and acting and thinking in ways that are consistent with this rational belief, then your emotions will assuredly change. Be patient! If you demand that your feelings change quickly after a few trials of what I outline in this chapter, you will quickly become discouraged and give up. Thus, do not expect to feel sadness or disappointment rather than depression until you have exercised your rational beliefs and associated constructive behaviour and realistic thinking on many occasions.

Another important ingredient in letting go of depression is to generalize your learning across situations. Earlier in this chapter, I encouraged you to identify the themes that underpin events about which you make yourself depressed (e.g. rejection, disapproval, failure to achieve your goals, blocks to autonomous living). Once you have confronted the prospect of being rejected in one situation, for example (while rehearsing a rational belief and acting and thinking in ways that are consistent with this belief), seek out other situations in which you think you may be rejected and practise the healthy belief–behaviour–thinking process while concentrating on being rejected. Even if you are not rejected in any given situation, you have gained valuable practice at handling such rejection in a healthy fashion.

Step 13 Deal with obstacles to making progress

Letting go of depression is not as straightforward a process as you might imagine having read this chapter this far. Indeed, it is fraught with difficulty, and you will either wittingly or unwittingly probably prevent yourself from making progress at becoming relatively free from depression in a number of ways. Why will you probably do this? Simply, as I first mentioned in Chapter 2, because you are human and humans frequently get in their own way while carrying out personal change programmes. I will now outline ways of overcoming some of the common obstacles to making progress in dealing with depression.

Overcoming Obstacle 1 Accept yourself for creating obstacles to progress

Once you have recognized that you have been stopping yourself in some way from doing what you need to do to let go of depression, then it is important that you accept yourself as a fallible human being who is not exempt from defeating himself. If you put yourself down for erecting hurdles to your progress, you are in fact demanding that you absolutely should not do what it is natural for humans to do: stop themselves in some way from continuing to work productively to let go of depression. It would be nice if demanding that you do not defeat yourself would in fact make it impossible for you to do so, but in reality this will not happen. Indeed, placing such demands on yourself only serves to create an additional, more pernicious obstacle, since, when you are demanding that you must not defeat yourself, you are not only preventing yourself from understanding how you are stopping yourself from letting go of depression and thereby from dealing effectively with this obstacle, but are creating a second emotional problem, e.g. depression, shame or anger at yourself for 'falling off the wagon'. To tackle this problem, it is important that you accept yourself unconditionally as a person who has done the wrong thing, rather than as a stupid person who absolutely should not have defeated himself in the first place. Doing this will help you get back on track.

Overcoming Obstacle 2 Learning that understanding is not enough

Once you have learned about and understood the dynamics of depression and the steps you need to take to let go of this debilitating emotion, you may think that this understanding is sufficient for you to achieve this goal. Sadly, as with anxiety, it is not. In this chapter, I have outlined a number of skills to help you to identify, challenge and change the irrational beliefs that underpin your depression, and to act and think in ways that are consistent with the alternative rational beliefs that underpin sadness and disappointment, which I see as healthy emotional responses to loss and failure respectively. Understanding what these skills are is an important first step to using them, since if you do not know what these skills are you will not be able to practise them. However, and this is the crucial point, understanding what these skills are does not help you to internalize them. Only concerted and repeated practice will help you do this, and unless you get your hands dirty, so to speak, by using these skills in real life, all the understanding in the world will not help you to let go of depression.

So, regard understanding as an important prelude to taking effective action, but see clearly that it is only that, a prelude. The key to letting go of depression, as I have reiterated throughout this chapter, is to repeatedly confront situations where you may experience loss or failure while rehearsing rational beliefs and acting and thinking in ways that are consistent with these rational beliefs. Learning that this is what you need to do is important, but won't, on its own, help you. *Acting* on this principle will.

Overcoming Obstacle 3 Don't act on the Magnus Magnusson principle

Mastermind was a very popular quiz programme, the quizmaster of which was Magnus Magnusson. If the buzzer indicating the end of a round sounded just after he had started asking a question, he would say, 'I've started, so I'll finish.' When applied to depression, the 'Magnus Magnusson principle', as I call it, refers to the tendency where once you have started depressing yourself by holding irrational beliefs and acting and thinking in ways that are consistent with these irrational beliefs, you continue to do so. If you act on this principle, you think that once you have started to depress yourself it is too late to do anything about it.

In reality, if you have a problem with depression it is important to accept the grim fact that even if you implement the guidelines outlined in this chapter, you will still begin to depress yourself at times. However, when you do, instead of finishing what you started, you can use the beginnings of an episode of depression to use these guidelines to work to un-depress yourself. This is the best way to refrain from acting on the Magnus Magnusson principle.

Overcoming Obstacle 4 Learn that depression is a sign of disturbance, not a sign of sensitivity

Some people think that depression is a sign of sensitivity, and as such they think that working towards becoming relatively free from depression means losing their sensitivity. It is therefore not surprising that these people resist using the guidelines outlined in this chapter. If you think that your feelings of depression are evidence of a great sensitivity, you are mistaken, for they are not. They are, in fact, evidence of disturbed oversensitivity. Depression, as I have stressed in this chapter, stems from rigid and extreme beliefs and is a sign that you are disturbing yourself about a loss or a failure. When you hold such beliefs you are saying in effect that 'It is terrible to have experienced the loss which I will not be able to recover from. My future is bleak and I have lost my capacity for happiness and fulfilment. This loss not only diminishes my life irrevocably, but also diminishes my worth as a person.'

Feelings of sadness when you have experienced a loss and

feelings of disappointment when you have failed are signs that you care about what you have lost or about failing at an important goal. These feelings are negative, but they are healthy and stem from flexible and non-extreme beliefs where you are saying, in effect, 'I care about what I have lost (for example), but this loss is not the end of my life. I need to mourn this loss, but I can conceive of a future and I acknowledge that I haven't lost my capacity for happiness and fulfilment. This loss diminishes my life temporarily, but does not diminish my worth as a person.'

I hope the above makes the point that sadness and disappointment are signs of non-disturbed sensitivity, while depression indicates a disturbed oversensitivity. Accept this and you will overcome this obstacle to letting go of depression.

Overcoming Obstacle 5 Go against the strong urge to escape from harsh reality by going to sleep

When you decide to pursue your goals and face up to the fact that you may fail or experience losses along the way, you may still short-circuit your progress by going along with your strong urge to escape from reality when it becomes harsh. This is why sleeping is so attractive to you when you have begun to make yourself depressed. First of all, going to bed allows you to withdraw from the aversive events of your life, and second, it is physically comforting. While comforting yourself is important for you when you are depressed, inactive comforts do tend to make it easier for you to maintain your negative, depressed mindset. This is where sleep comes in. It allows you to escape, not only from the world but from your own depressive thoughts. However, it is important that you avoid excessive sleeping when you are depressed, no matter how appealing it is to you. First, sleeping is inactive, and as 'depression thrives on inactivity', you are unwittingly creating far more problems for yourself in the longer term than you solve in the short term. Second, sleeping is a form of withdrawal, and as such it reinforces your irrational beliefs about loss or failure which led you to feel depressed and withdraw in the first place. Third, excessive sleeping actually makes you more tired. You then think that as you are tired you need more sleep, and therefore sleep far longer than you need to. You actually need less sleep when you feel tiredness that is associated with depression. Fourth, excessive sleeping, as a form of withdrawal, severely disrupts your sleep patterns and can lead to insomnia (i.e. not sleeping when you 'should': at night).

It is therefore very important that you recognize that 'taking to your bed' and going to sleep only helps you in the very short term and, in fact, serves only to deepen your depression in the longer term. Instead, use the techniques outlined in this book to deal with what you are depressed about. In doing so, you will be taking an active stance towards self-help, which is a good antidote to depression.

As I said earlier in this section, part of the reason why you 'take to your bed' when you have begun to make yourself feel depressed is to comfort yourself. I noted in passing that self-comfort is important when you are depressed. However, it is important that you find ways of comforting yourself which (1) do not stop you from using the REBT self-help skills that I have described in this book and (2) are based on an active, compassionate stance towards tackling your depression. The 'active' in active compassion is important because activity makes it harder for 'depression to thrive', and the 'compassion' part is important because it reinforces the importance of adopting a caring, understanding and self-helping attitude towards yourself.

An excellent way of putting this principle of active compassion into practice is by taking regular exercise. Such exercise is important for a number of reasons. First, it helps you counter the inactivity you are more naturally drawn to when you have begun to depress yourself. Second, it demonstrates that you care for yourself by doing your best to ensure that you have a healthy body. Third, it helps you to develop and sustain a good level of energy that will make it easier for you to develop a healthy mind by implementing the procedures that I have discussed in this book. Finally, regular exercise will aid you in developing a non-depressed world view, which I will now briefly outline and discuss.

Step 14 Develop and rehearse a non-depressed world view

As I mentioned in the previous chapter, we develop views of the world as it relates to us that make it more or less likely that we will experience unhealthy positive emotions. The world views that render you vulnerable to depression do so primarily because they draw your attention to the negative and lead you to edit out the positive and because they emphasize the 'intolerable' nature of suffering. In this final section, I discuss the importance of developing realistic views of the world that will help you let go of depression. I will present an illustrative rather than exhaustive list of such world views, to help you to develop your own. What I will do first is to describe a world view that renders you vulnerable to depression and then give its healthy alternative. You will see that the latter is characterized by its complexity and non-extreme nature, whereas, in the former, aspects of the world that relate to loss or failure are portrayed as unidimensional and extreme.

Views of the world that render you vulnerable to depression	**Views of the world that help you to let go of depression**
The world is a bad place.	The world is a place where bad, good and neutral things happen.
Life is ultimately meaningless.	Life neither has meaning nor is meaningless. I can find and actively pursue a number of meaningful projects over my life span.
People will ultimately reject me, therefore it is best not to get involved with them.	Some people will reject me, others will not. I can actively involve myself in relationships in light of this fact.
People cannot be trusted.	People vary enormously along a continuum of trustworthiness. My best stance is to trust someone unless I have evidence to the contrary. If I am let down that is very unfortunate, but hardly terrible, and won't unduly affect my stance towards the next person I meet.
The world is made up of strong and weak people.	The world is made up of people who all have their strengths and weaknesses.

If you hold rational beliefs that are consistent with the views of the world listed on the right-hand side of the above table and if you act and think in ways that are, in turn, consistent with these rational beliefs, then doing all this will help you to let go of depression.

HOW ROBERTA LET GO OF DEPRESSION

In this closing section, I will tell the story of Roberta, who used the principles in this book to help herself let go of her sociotropic depression (see page 62 for a full discussion of autonomous and sociotropic depression). Once again, to preserve her confidentiality, I have changed any identifying details. Like Phil, who I discussed at the end of Chapter 2, Roberta was a client of mine and thus used the principles with my counselling help.

Roberta, a 25-year-old housewife, became depressed when her husband of five years left her for another woman. They had no children. Roberta's depression centred on three major issues, as we shall see. First, she considered that her husband leaving her for another woman meant that she was unlovable. Second, she considered that she was too weak to cope on her own without a man to look after her. Third, she felt sorry for herself for losing her relationship through no fault of her own. She was referred to me by a psychiatrist who saw her after she took an overdose. Here is how Roberta progressed through the 14 steps that I described above.

Step 1 Roberta admits that she experiences depression and that it is a problem for her

Right from the beginning, Roberta freely admitted that she suffered from depression and that it was a problem for her.

Step 2 Roberta sees that sadness is a viable alternative to depression

Initially, Roberta had difficulty in understanding that she could feel anything but depressed about being rejected by her husband and being left to cope on her own. It was only when I explained what her three basic options were that she began to see that there was an alternative to feeling depressed. I showed her that her three options were: (1) to believe that it didn't matter if her husband rejected her or not (indifference); (2) to believe that it was the end of the world to be rejected by her husband and that there was no hope for her (horror); or (3) to believe that it was tragic to be rejected by her husband, but not the end of the world, and that after an appropriate period of mourning she could construct a new life for herself (transcendable tragedy). Roberta could see straight away that the indifference option was ridiculous, that her own reaction was based on the horror option and that while she would like to choose the transcendable tragedy option, she doubted that she could ever believe it. Eventually, she saw that whether or not she could believe the transcendable tragedy option was not the point at this stage. The main point was that she would like to believe it, and if she did she would feel profound sadness, but not depression, about the loss of her husband.

Step 3 Roberta accepts herself for feeling depression

Although Roberta considered herself to be weak and unable to cope without a man, she did not depreciate herself for feeling depressed. Thus, we did not have any work to do on this step.

Step 4 Roberta lists the situations in which she felt depressed and identifies themes

Roberta felt depressed in the following situations:

- whenever she saw a happily married couple, in real life or in the media;
- going out to situations where she was on her own and others were in couples;
- when something went wrong in her house that she couldn't fix;
- listening to other women talking about how well their partners looked after them;
- when she went to bed on her own.

In considering these situations with me, Roberta identified the following themes that were present in her depression:

- being aware that she was on her own;
- being aware that she had no one to look after her.

Step 5 Roberta identifies her general loss-related irrational beliefs and their emotional, behavioural and thinking consequences

Roberta's depression was partly ego-based and partly non-ego-based. She had three major general loss-related irrational beliefs, and I list these below, together with their emotional, behavioural and thinking consequences:

Roberta's general loss-related irrational belief: ego-based	**Consequences of GiB**
My husband absolutely should not have left me and I am unlovable because he did.	– Predicting that nobody else will want me – Picturing myself alone and miserable in the future – Withdrawing from people, especially couples, whenever I can – Turning down invitations from my single friends to go out socially where I may meet men

Roberta's general loss-related irrational beliefs: non-ego-based	**Consequences of GiB**
I must have a man in my life to look after me and if I don't I can't bear it.	– Feeling depressed when I think that I am on my own without a man to look after me – Thinking about all the things that may go wrong in my life that I couldn't deal with – Picturing myself alone and miserable in the future – Seeking help from men I am not interested in, since I am scared of being rejected by men that I am interested in – Not trying to do tasks around the house which my husband did because I think I cannot do them

I did nothing to deserve my husband leaving me for someone else and therefore this absolutely should not have happened to me. The world is a horrible place for allowing such unfairness to exist. Poor me!	– Feeling depressed when thinking about the unfair way I have been treated – Constantly thinking about how unfairly I have been treated – Thinking that it is not worth trying to met someone else because I will only be treated unfairly again – Talking about how unfairly I have been treated with my friends and anyone else who will listen – Reading about other women who have been treated badly by their husbands

Step 6 Roberta challenges her general loss-related irrational beliefs, then develops and rehearses an alternative set of general rational beliefs

Roberta used the following guidelines to challenge her three general loss-related irrational beliefs and replace them with three alternative rational beliefs.

1 State your general irrational belief.
2 Give reasons why your general irrational belief is irrational.
3 State the alternative general rational belief.
4 Give reasons why your general rational belief is rational.

I will just present here the work that Roberta did on the following GiB: 'I did nothing to deserve my husband leaving me for someone else and therefore this absolutely should not have happened to me. The world is a horrible place for allowing such unfairness to exist. Poor me!'

1 State your general loss-related irrational belief:

I did nothing to deserve my husband leaving me for someone else and therefore this absolutely should not have happened to me. The world is a horrible place for allowing such unfairness to exist. Poor me!

2 Give reasons why this general irrational belief is irrational:

It is not true that while I did nothing to deserve my husband leaving me for someone else, therefore this absolutely should not have happened to me. There is no law that dictates that I must not be treated in an undeserving manner. If there was then it would have been impossible for my husband to have left me for someone else. The fact that he did just this is evidence that no such law exists. Furthermore, it is not the case that the world is a horrible place for allowing such unfairness to exist. If it was then only bad things could happen in the world, which is obviously not the case. Finally, I am not a poor person who needs to be pitied. If I was, only unfairness could happen to me. Again, this is not true.

If I believe that because I did nothing to deserve my husband leaving me for someone else, therefore this great unfairness absolutely should not have happened to me, I will feel depressed and sorry for myself and not do anything constructive to help myself.

3 State the alternative general rational belief:

It may be the case that I did nothing to deserve my husband leaving me for someone else, and while I would have preferred that this did not happen to me, that doesn't mean that it absolutely should not have happened. There is no law that states that I am immune from being treated in an undeserving way. The world is not a terrible place for 'permitting' this to happen. Rather, it is an enormously complex place where both fairness and unfairness happen, as well as events that have nothing to do with the domain of fairness and unfairness. Finally, I am not a poor person for being treated in an undeserving way. I am a non-poor person who is in a poor situation.

4 Give reasons why your general rational belief is rational:

First, it is true that I would have preferred it if my husband had not left me for someone else, and it is also true that I am not immune from being treated in this undeserved manner. Second, it is true that the world is an enormously complex place where both fairness and unfairness happen, as well as events that have nothing to do with the domain of fairness and unfairness. The fact that I have been treated unfairly by my husband is a reflection of this fact. Finally, it is true that I am a non-poor person who is in a poor situation. As such, I can point to many occasions where I have been in very good situations.

If I held this general rational belief, I would feel sad, but not depressed, about being unfairly left by my husband. Also, I would feel sorry about my plight, but not sorry for myself.

Roberta reviewed the above arguments regularly, and as she did so she rehearsed her general rational belief. As she came to really believe that she was not a person to be pitied but a person who, like everyone else in life, is not immune from being treated unfairly, she began to focus on getting her life together and stopped complaining about her plight to her friends and others. Her friends, as a result, found her more rewarding to be with.

She made similar progress on her other two general loss-related irrational beliefs. Thus, she began to see that she could still be lovable even though her husband had left her for another woman. As a result she started to go to social events with her friends and lost her fear of meeting men.

Finally, she began to accept that she didn't need looking after by a man and that she could learn to do a lot of things that her husband had done for her. Thus, instead of asking her male friends to do jobs around the house for her, she asked them to teach her how to do them for herself.

Step 7 Roberta analyses specific episodes of depression

Roberta used the ABC framework described earlier in this chapter to deal with a number of specific episodes where she felt depressed about her husband leaving her for another woman. Here is an ABC that Roberta did of a specific episode when she felt depressed about this.

Situation

I went to a dinner party tonight where the couples there seemed very happy together.

A = Activating event

I was most depressed about being on my own at the party.

Since it was true that Roberta was on her own at the party, she did not have to assume that her A was factual (see page 68). It was!

B* = *Irrational belief

I absolutely should not have been alone tonight and the fact that I was proves that I am unlovable.

C* = *Consequences of the irrational beliefs at B about the activating event at A

Emotional C = Depression

Behavioural C = Going to bed and staying there for two days.

Thinking C = Thinking that I will always be on my own.

Step 8 Roberta challenges her specific loss-related irrational beliefs, then develops and rehearses an alternative set of specific rational beliefs

Roberta used the following guidelines to challenge her specific loss-related irrational belief and replace it with an alternative specific rational belief.

1 State your general irrational belief.
2 Give reasons why your general irrational belief is irrational.
3 State the alternative general rational belief.
4 Give reasons why your general rational belief is rational.

1 State your specific loss-related irrational belief:

I absolutely should not have been alone tonight and the fact that I was proves that I am unlovable.

2 Give reasons why this specific irrational belief is irrational:

While it would have been highly desirable for me not to have been on my own at the dinner party tonight, there is no law decreeing that I absolutely should have been with my husband. If there were, he would have been with me tonight. He wasn't and therefore no such law exists. Also, it is not true that I am unlovable. My husband leaving me for another woman means that he was unhappy with me, but not that I am unlovable. If I were unlovable, I would not be able to be loved and this is not true. I have been loved in the past and the chances are I will be loved again. It is illogical for me to conclude that one event, albeit a very significant one, like my husband leaving me, can define me as unlovable. This is the part–whole error. Finally, as long as I believe that I absolutely should not have been on my own tonight and that I am unlovable because I was, I will feel depressed, withdraw and think that I will always be on my own.

3 State the alternative specific rational belief:

I really wish that I was not on my own tonight, but that doesn't mean that I absolutely should have been with my husband. The fact that I wasn't proves that I am the same person with or without my husband. I am not unlovable.

4 Give reasons why this specific rational belief is rational:

It is true that I really wish that I was not on my own tonight and also true that there is no law stating that I absolutely should have been with my husband. This full preference is consistent with what happened tonight. It is also true that I am the same person whether I am with my husband or without him. My 'lovability' is constant as long as I am alive, fallible and unique. Holding this rational belief will help me to feel sad, but not depressed, about my loss. As such I will not withdraw and go to bed. Rather, I will stay involved with life and acknowledge that while I might not meet anyone immediately, I will probably meet someone – if I want to – relatively soon.

Roberta reviewed the above arguments after coming back from the party, and as a result she went out the next day and reminded herself that it was unlikely she would end up alone in life (see the next step).

Step 9 Roberta mourns her loss and then gets on with life, while rehearsing rational beliefs and while thinking realistically and acting healthily

Roberta followed the general guidance about mourning her loss that I discussed earlier in this chapter. Roberta allowed herself to feel sad and to acknowledge that, while she had been treated unfairly, complaining about this to all and sundry would make it much harder for her to move on with life. So she stopped doing so and asked her friends to dissuade her from complaining should she start to do so. She also gradually accepted their invitations to go out socially. As she reintegrated herself into social life, she rehearsed her specific rational beliefs and acted and thought in ways that were consistent with these specific beliefs. In order to determine what were constructive ways of acting and thinking, she re-did her situational ABCs, this time based on holding a specific rational belief. For example, here is how she re-did her situational ABC about being on her own at the dinner party. Note her new behavioural C and new thinking C.

Situation

I went to a dinner party tonight where the couples there seemed very happy together.

A = Activating event

Being on my own at the party.

B = Rational belief

I really wish that I was not on my own tonight, but that doesn't mean that I absolutely should have been with my husband. The fact that I wasn't proves that I am the same person with or without my husband. I am not unlovable.

C = Consequences of the rational beliefs at B about the activating event at A

Emotional C = Sadness

Behavioural C = Staying out of bed and going out the next day.

Thinking C = Thinking that I will probably meet someone before long.

As you can see, behaviourally Roberta stayed out of bed and went out the next day instead of going to bed for two days. Thinking-wise, she realized that her thought that she would end up alone in life was unrealistic and a function of her irrational belief, and instead she acknowledged that she would probably meet someone before long if she wanted to.

Step 10 Roberta confronts potential losses and failures in her mind's eye and then in reality

As Roberta made progress in counselling and started to become less vulnerable to depression, she began to integrate herself into social life and to take responsibility for her own life. To help her do this, I taught her to use the imagery technique that I described on page 30. Thus, she prepared herself to feel sad, but not depressed, about being rejected by any men that she might meet. She also used the technique to feel disappointed, but not depressed, about any failure she experienced in tackling tasks that she had previously allowed her husband to do for her, tasks such as changing a plug, hanging pictures on the wall and painting walls.

Roberta followed up this imagery practice by taking sensible risks in real life concerning meeting new men and tackling household tasks. In doing this, she rehearsed appropriate rational beliefs and constructive behaviours and realistic thinking that were consistent with these rational beliefs. Thus, she practised acting and thinking like an independent woman who wanted, but did not need, a man in her life, either to prove her lovability or to take care of her and protect her from the tedious aspects of life. As she confronted and dealt with possible losses and failures in life in both imagination and, more importantly, in reality, Roberta developed a psychological resilience that would help her to let go of depression.

Step 11 Roberta deals with the thinking consequences of irrational beliefs

Once Roberta had developed a reasonable level of conviction in her rational beliefs, she noticed, like Phil whose story I told at the end of Chapter 2, that her subsequent thinking became more realistic. Thus, as she accepted that she didn't need to rely on a man, she realized that she might be more competent than she previously thought at doing routine household tasks. Also, as she began to accept that she was not immune from being treated unfairly, she concluded that it was not inevitable that all men would teat her unfairly in the future. Instead, she more realistically saw that different men would treat her in different ways – a stance that helped her to decide that she was perhaps ready to begin dating again.

However, Roberta found that disputing her irrational belief that she was unlovable for being rejected by her husband, who she held absolutely should not have left her, did not by itself shift her prediction that nobody would truly want her in future, nor her image of herself ending up alone and miserable. She dealt with her negative prediction about not being wanted in the future in two ways. First, she labelled this thought as reflecting the thinking error of 'negative prediction' and then developed the following healthy antidote based on a 'realistic prediction': 'It is likely that some men may want me even though this may take some time.'

She wrote each thought on a 5x3 card, like this:

'Nobody else will want me.'	'It is likely that some men may want me, even though this may take some time.'

Then she asked herself the following questions:

1 Which of these two thoughts is the more realistic?
2 If a friend had a similar experience, which of these two ways of thinking would I encourage my friend to adopt?

This helped her to see that her negative prediction was the unrealistic thought. Second, if this thought still came to her mind even though she had concluded that it was unrealistic, she allowed it to come into her mind and allowed it to leave again without engaging with it. Furthermore, she found that the more she acted according to the more realistic thought that she would find someone else who would want her even though this would probably take some time, the less the thought 'Nobody will want me' came to mind. Roberta thus used a combination of Options 2 and 3 in dealing with this thinking consequence of her irrational belief about being rejected by her husband.

With respect to her image of ending up alone and miserable, Roberta used the ambitious Option 5. Thus, she first assumed that she wouldn't find another man. Then, she showed herself that she could still be happy in life without a man, although she would perhaps be happier with one in her life. She wrote down all the activities that she could engage in without a man that she would find meaningful and pleasurable, and every time she had the image of herself ending up alone and miserable she pictured herself being alone and happy.

Step 12 Roberta commits herself to confront loss and failure on a regular basis and to generalize her learning

As counselling continued, Roberta increasingly took responsibility for her life. She learned more and more skills in the home and began to explore interests that she had always wanted to pursue but was too scared. She rehearsed her new rational belief that if she failed at anything, this would be unfortunate, but would only prove that she was a fallible human being who can succeed and fail at things.

As she began to see that life could be enjoyable and meaningful without a man, Roberta became more discerning about the men she went out with. Before, she had gone out with men who she saw as strong and who would look after her. When she found such a man she would tolerate being badly treated by him because she considered that she needed to have him in her life. Now, because she increasingly saw that she could look after herself, she went out with men who would show respect for her, and when they started to take her for granted she asserted herself with them, ending relationships if they continued to neglect her.

Step 13 Roberta deals with her obstacles to making progress

Roberta had two major obstacles to making progress in letting go of her anxiety. First, Roberta resisted the idea that she could help herself. This was consistent with her belief that she needed to rely on a man to help her. As a male counsellor, I was well aware that Roberta would take a passive role as a client. Given this, I raised it as an issue at the beginning of counselling, and agreed with Roberta that I would bring this to her attention and we would then conduct behavioural experiments to determine whether or not she could do what she thought she couldn't do. Most of the time Roberta surprised herself by being able to do what she thought she couldn't do. This referred to the thinking and behavioural exercises that I have discussed throughout this book. As Roberta developed the idea that she could be competent in life and didn't need a man to help her, she took increasing responsibility for her therapy and became far less reliant on me to help her.

The second obstacle to change that Roberta encountered was what I have called the Magnus Magnusson principle – 'I've started, so I'll finish.' Thus, Roberta thought that when she felt depressed then it was too late to do anything to help herself. Instead, I taught her that an early sign of depression could be seen as a cue to self-help based on the ideas presented in this book. So, whenever Roberta began to feel depressed, she would do an ABC analysis on her feelings and would then dispute the irrational belief that underpinned her depressive experience. Rather than seeing depression as a sign that it was too late to help herself, Roberta began to act on the anti-Magnus Magnusson principle: just because I have begun to depress myself, it doesn't mean that I have to continue to do so. Rather, I can see depression as a sign that I can begin to help myself.

Roberta also used the anti-Magnus Magnusson principle to stop herself from acting on her urge to get men to do things around the house for her. Thus, she distinguished between experiencing the urge to portray herself as helpless in front of a man, in order for him to rescue her, and acting on this urge. I also showed her that if she actually asked a man to do something that it was in her interests for her to do herself, she could change her mind after the words were out of her mouth, so that even if she started adopting the helpless role, she didn't have to continue in this role. In this way, Roberta put up with the short-term discomfort of learning to be independent around the house in order to develop a sense of competence and then confidence in her resourcefulness. Tackling this and her other obstacles to change helped Roberta to let go of her depression.

Step 14 Roberta's new non-depressed world view

Based on the work that Roberta and I did on her problems in counselling, Roberta let go of her depression about being rejected by her husband and about dealing with life without relying on a man. She came to see that she was lovable whether she had a man in her life or not, and that she was quite capable of doing many of the things which she had looked towards men to do for her.

As a result, Roberta developed the following non-depressed world view that was relevant to her problems, which I contrast with her previous depressed world view. Acting on her new non-depressed world view and the rational beliefs that were a central part of it helped Roberta to let go of her depression and to live a richer life than she would have lived if her husband had not rejected her.

Roberta's depressed world view	**Roberta's non-depressed world view**
My life revolves around having a man in my life.	My life may be enhanced by having a man in my life, but it does not depend on this. Having a man is not necessary to my life, it is a desirable optional extra.
Men will ultimately reject me, therefore it is best not to get involved with them.	Some men will reject me, others will not. I can actively involve myself in relationships in light of this fact.
Men cannot be trusted.	Men vary enormously along a continuum of trustworthiness. My best stance is to trust a man unless I have evidence to the contrary. If I am let down, that is very unfortunate but hardly terrible, and won't unduly affect my stance towards the next man I meet.
The world is made up of strong and weak people. I am a weak person.	The world is made up of people who all have their strengths and weaknesses, and this includes me.

We have now reached the end of the book. I hope that you will use the ideas that I have presented in this book to help yourself let go of anxiety or depression or both. Remember, if you are going to be successful at this, passively reading the book isn't sufficient. You will have to put these ideas into practice and do so repeatedly. Good luck!

Index